journey - approach
Much later,

\ was
10/12/1995

Discovering the
Royal Child
Within

Discovering the Royal Child Within

A Spiritual Psychology of *The Little Prince*

ᗑ

Eugen Drewermann

Translated by Peter Heinegg

CROSSROAD • NEW YORK

1993

The Crossroad Publishing Company
370 Lexington Avenue, New York, NY 10017

Originally published under the title *Das Eigentliche ist unsichtbar:
Der Kleine Prinz tiefenpsychologisch gedeutet*
© Verlag Herder Freiburg im Breisgau 1984

English translation copyright © 1993 by
The Crossroad Publishing Company

Printed in the United States of America

Library of Congress Cataloging-in-Publication Data

Drewermann, Eugen.
[Eigentliche ist unsichtbar. English]
Discovering the royal child within : a spiritual psychology of
"The little prince" / Eugen Drewermann ; translated by Peter
Heinegg.
p. cm.
Translation of: Das Eigentliche ist unsichtbar : Der Kleine Prinz
tiefenpsychologisch gedeutet
Includes bibliographical references.
ISBN 0-8245-1267-7 (pbk.)
1. Saint Exupéry, Antoine de, 1900–1944. Petit prince.
2. Princes and princesses in literature. 3. Spiritual life in
literature. 4. Psychology in literature. 5. Children in
literature. I. Title.
PQ2637.A274P4613 1993
843'.912–dc20   92-45230
                                                      CIP

Contents

ℭℬ

5

Part Two
QUESTIONS AND ANALYSES

Preface

CR

FOR COUNTLESS twentieth-century readers Antoine de Saint-Exupéry's masterpiece, his fairy tale *The Little Prince,* has become the narrative key to their life. The book has provided them with a place of refuge in times of loneliness, comfort in hours of disappointment, and hope in moments of abandonment. *The Little Prince* has been an indispensable companion on the often long roads of seeking and longing; and its subdued sadness has proved to be a source of warmth and understanding in an increasingly cold world.

Is it the eternal dream of lost childhood that makes *The Little Prince* so comforting and sympathetic? Certainly, but there's more to it than that. There is also the artful, ironic liberation it offers from the crazy, compulsive world of "big people" — a pause to catch one's breath in the human desert. But above all *The Little Prince* can go a good way toward restoring trust in the unconditional fidelity of love. It promises and embodies a world of striving and mutual responsibility; and it shows a solidarity in love that is unconquerable, even in death. It is a hymn to friendship

7

and camaraderie in images of bewitching simplicity and beauty.

No wonder Saint-Exupéry's *Little Prince* has acquired the status of an ideal dream figure of humanity. Its insight into the kingdom of children's innocence, and still more its view of the stars, which ring like bells in the night, telling us about the invisible planet of an extraordinary rose, restore to us a breadth of the heart and a depth of dreaming that we thought well-nigh lost in the dreariness of our days. Involuntarily, with an almost maternal sympathy, we find ourselves wishing that the Little Prince will be happy and safe in his little astral world, almost forgetting that in Saint-Exupéry's work he is "dead" to this world for an uncertain period. We wish Saint-Exupéry himself had been able to realize the figure of the Little Prince in his own life; and we're only too ready to believe the large number of biographers who assure us that in the likeness of the Little Prince their friend and comrade Antoine has bequeathed to posterity a portrait of himself.

It is, in fact, indispensable to apply depth psychology to the clearly autobiographical features of *The Little Prince.* Of course, this risks destroying the Saint-Exupéry myth. But it simply won't do to "protect" him by removing from his person the pervasive contradictions of his life and *oeuvre:* They can't just be blamed on the troubled times he lived in. But if we maintain our objectivity we have a chance of encountering Saint-Exupéry in *The Little Prince* more profoundly and revealingly than in all his other wonderful writings.

In Saint-Exupéry's work there are many passages where we have to understand him rather than believe him. Some readers may feel like turning away, in disappointed love or offended sympathy, from the view presented here, which has thus far yet to appear in literary criticism. Right from the start I must assure any such readers that the concerns and statements of a writer as great as Saint-Exupéry can never be understood unless we "transcend" them. We have to bring to them the sense of, or rather the faith and confidence in, a dimension of reality that presents itself as still more lovable, hopeful, comforting, and human than anything Saint-Exupéry himself may have been able to see from the height of his vision of the world.

Saint-Exupéry's work has the greatness and value of a prophetic call — but the greatest of the prophets were ultimately refuted in their message when people got around to following them: When the storm wind from the prophets' mouths abated, God always spoke in the soft voice of "sheer silence" (1 Kings 19:12), which wanted not strenuous effort but kindness. The Little Prince will return to this world only if we help to point up and overcome the contradictions on which he came to grief. The Little Prince must be allowed to live, here on this earth — that is the central goal of this theological-psychological essay. I want to go on dreaming, through words and images, the rich, dense symbols in Saint-Exupéry's famous story.

Introduction

߷

ANYONE WHO TRIES TO INTERPRET *The Little Prince* is subject to the danger of turning into a baobab or "monkey bread tree." Baobabs are like that: With their bloated colossal proportions they destroy every secret planet of happiness. They uproot the world of children and churn up the world of dreams. With the polyp-like growths of their insatiable trains of thought they worm their way through every holy ground from which the beauty of a rose might spring. Doesn't any interpretation, especially a psychological one, kill the language of poetry? It kills its immediacy and replaces it with reflection. It kills its warmth and emotional depth and replaces them with stratospheric conceptual flights of hypothesis and abstraction. It murders the concentrated unity of a symbolic overview, dissolving it in analysis and dissection. "If you want to understand people, you mustn't listen to what they say."[1]

Why then should we bother with a psychological interpretation of *The Little Prince?* Why not just let the images simply be themselves in their simple meaning? Because, it

11

must be said, every real literary work condenses a complex reality into a multilayered symbol. We understand the language of literature only in a peculiar mixture of empathetic observation and reflective analysis.

It's true: We can destroy the imaginative power and binding force of any dreamlike poetic or religious image, by breaking it down into its constituent parts and thus creating an intellectual distance that makes all immediate feeling wither and die. But the reverse is also true: A poetic narrative or a dream can be robbed of its reality and effectiveness by treating it as we usually do on waking up in the morning. We smile, uneasily or amusedly, at the dream messages from the night before, and note to our relief that the whole thing was just a dream.[2] Or in a playful narrative mood we retell the dream images to our friends, without rediscovering ourselves in them or paying attention to their painfully clear diagnostic implications. Finally we can also use our own dreams to flee from reality. For intellectuals, the world of literature can at any time take on a narcotic function, and every reading of real literature that does not prompt the reader to self-examination fails in its peculiar function.

Thus there is no avoiding interpretation, and the reader isn't automatically changed into a "baobab" of presumptive self-superiority just by reflecting on what piece of reality has "gelled" in a piece of literature. Clearly there is a characteristic difference between interpretation of literature that looks to the real life condensed within it and a scholarly, purely literary critique. The latter seeks to analyze the linguistic means by which life has been reshaped into literature. We by contrast are concerned with describing the reality itself that is condensed and expressed in a literary (or representational) work of art. We're interested not so much in the artistic value of the literary work as in the psychic and existential truth it contains.

Since Saint-Exupéry himself said of analysis: "Logic exists on a level with things, and not with the knot that it ties,"[3] it is indispensable to see just how far we ourselves can recognize the binding force of that "knot," of the concentrating vision, of the creation of poetic meaning beyond the knot. Everything Saint-Exupéry wrote had something visionary about it; his work presents itself as a kind of mission to humanity. This makes it all the more important to ask: What are the experiences and findings, motives and goals, the personal impressions and events, the human evidence that have left their mark on the work of this writer? No doubt, "The creator always withdraws from his creation. And the trace he leaves behind is pure logic."[4] But if a literary creation wants to have an impact, we need to ask about the image of humanity that lives within it, and about the person who finds his or her likeness fashioned in it. Works of art have to be interpreted not because of some ineradicable desire for (psycho-) logical dissection, but because of a striving for existential truth.

There's another reason as well. Millions of people have read *The Little Prince;* millions more will eventually read it. A few centuries from now the gigantic libraries of our age (which continues to write books) might be crammed into a handful of characteristic "snapshots," the way we already use Dante's poetry as a shorthand expression for "the" Middle Ages, or Shakespeare's plays for "the" Elizabethan period. In that case it could be that just two works of literature will be considered essential to and characteristic of the twentieth century, shaken as it has been by bloody, all-consuming conflict: Franz Kafka's *The Castle* and Saint-Exupéry's *The Little Prince.*

As far as *The Castle* goes, there can be no doubt: In its uncanny way this novel offers the key to understanding the current crisis of determining what it means to be human. Nowhere else is the meaninglessness and alienation, the inner division and loneliness, the abandonment and lostness of our existence described more hauntingly.[5] Past ages may have been able to paint their self-portraits in myths and fairy tales, sagas and legends, but Kafka's novel is an anti-fairy tale, a cruel vision of entrapment in a dead-end within a cold, bureaucratic, incomprehensible, and unassailable world. Here even the metaphors of hope, the fairy tale images of the town and the castle, are transformed into symbols of woe. Hence it seems that we could call no better witness to rebut despair than the author of the counter-Castle, the "city in the wilderness," the "citadel" (*The Wisdom of the Sands*).[6] It's no accident that while people may not read the whole fragmented literary testament of Saint-Exupéry, they do hold on to *The Little Prince,* as a sort of breviary of hope, a vademecum of love. If anything could, *The Little Prince* evidently can serve as proof that even our confused century is capable of producing a fairy tale of transcendent value.

Thus, to examine this short book and to explore its psychic world means no more and no less than asking to what extent there is or can be any credible hope for humanity in our age, which has been so inhuman in so many ways. We sense that we live in an endlessly spreading desert, but the question is: Does it contain an oasis, and if so, where? Thus we shall have to join Saint-Exupéry on the path of the stars and cisterns. We shall have to see how much light we can find in the night and how much water in the desert. We have to try to understand his message, and test it to see how well it holds up.

Part One

☙

THE MESSAGE

Chapter 1

The Royal Child —
A Quasi-Religious Rediscovery

cs

I T'S AMAZING: Whenever writers have something crucial to say, they draw it from the wellspring of religious images. Such is the case with Saint-Exupéry's *Little Prince.*

All cultures tell of royal children who come to visit us from hidden parts of the globe, and who can see everything in a different light. This archetypal motif has an intrinsically religious quality to it. But Saint-Exupéry links up much more closely with the language of religion when he tells of a king's son who came from a distant star to appear in our midst. This royal child, he assures us, dwelt in our world for only a short time. Within a year death awaited him, and he had to return to the light of the stars. Still his coming wasn't in vain, because since then we may wait for his return, and in the darkness of night the stars shine down on us with a different light. The world hasn't changed since the Little Prince walked on it; but it's possible to see it through his eyes. And many things that we now take seriously will strike us as ridiculous, and vice versa. Some great things will seem base, some inconspicuous things will seem great; and many parts of our humanity that we have denied – especially dreaming, waiting, and loving – can be rediscovered.

What else connects religion to the figure of the "divine child" but our heart's need to find its way back to its origin? Or the desire for our life to begin once more as if born anew, surrounded by a world where animals talk, flowers speak, and stars sing, as in *The Little Prince?*

The New Testament doesn't really spell out what Jesus meant when he said to his disciples, "Unless you turn and become like children, you will never enter the kingdom of heaven" (Mt. 18:3). But even if we take care not to project certain romantic-radiant features into the condition of being a child,[1] we will still have to say that a "child," in the religious sense, manifests two attitudes enabling it never to deny its true essence: trust and loyalty.

From a religious standpoint "child" is a code word for a life borne up by an imperturbable trust in the goodness of what lies behind or beneath the world. For this reason the "child" doesn't need all the safeguards against anxiety that fundamentally form and deform the life of "grown-ups."

So long as people are anxious, they will be afraid of being "small." Fear will drive them on to become increasingly bigger and more "grown-up," until they outgrow their own proportions and become literally "puffed up":[2] arrogant and unreal behind the as-if facade[3] of never-ending but illusory talents and skills. In the Sermon on the Mount Jesus says, pleading with his audience and urging them to relax, "And which of you by being anxious can add one cubit to his span of life?" (Mt. 6:27). But in a state of anxiety it's impossible to live this truth. A "child" is a person who has learned to renounce the illusory world of the awful anxieties plaguing the "big shots," the boasters and show-offs, the chronically frightened propagators of fear. A "child" has learned, in a sense, to begin life anew: with the steadfast courage to seek the truth — because God's blessing rests only on truth, for those who accept it (Mt. 5:3) — and also with an endless longing for a world that is gentler, more peaceful, compassionate, and altogether more just (Mt. 5:5-9). Such a "child" won't let itself be blinded by the power, the thirst for glory, the careerism, and the money hunger of the "big people," because it knows that everything that is humanly true and serves peace is visible and accessible only to the "little ones" (Mt. 11:25). This feeling of trust makes it possible to be limitlessly open. The moral distinctions between good and evil, so important in the world of "grown-ups," may not hold for those who know about the illusory omnipotence of anxiety and loneliness, and who feel in their depths that they can be good only in the gift and happiness of love. Thus we hear Jesus saying in the New Testament that God makes the sun shine and the rain fall on both the just and the unjust (Mt. 6:45). The infinite God has to bend down equally far to all people, from the highest to the lowest, and every single one of them lives solely on God's grace.

The kind of "child" like Jesus might do a miracle one morning on Temple Square. He might reach a legally sanctioned lynching party about to stone an adulteress and get them to abandon, for the moment, their arrogant self-righteousness. He might get them to stop condemning her and to take the risk of looking into their own hearts (John 8:1-11). In the figure of Prince Myshkin (from *The Idiot*) Fyodor Dostoyevsky describes a similarly wonderful child, who stands far apart from the prejudices and condemnation of the Swiss villagers as he sides with the violated, outlawed, dying girl Marie. And Myshkin teaches the local children, who initially joined the adults in taunting her, to have immediate kindness and boundless understanding.[4] The love of such "children" is universal — it excludes nothing, be it human or beast, high or low, that is in need of help.

For "grown-ups" *social distinctions* are supremely important. The most critical point in their eyes is what sort of house you have, what kind of car you drive, and whether you know the right cutlery to use with fish or lobster. A "child" like Jesus didn't care whether his disciples washed their hands before or after dinner. He wanted to know what went on in people's hearts, what thoughts and feelings they harbored within themselves (Mk. 7:1–13). In a quite similar vein Georges Bernanos evokes this sort of child in the person of his country priest. The curé of Ambricourt helps the noble Madame de Chantal, who has been inconsolably mourning the death of her son and desperately quarreling with God. He restores her child to her by awakening in her the sense of a deeper security in God.[5]

A "child" is religious if he or she has overcome fear of people through trust in God. Those who at some point in their lives can believe in God as their father are, religiously speaking, "children of God." We can encounter such people as brothers or sisters in kindness with no ulterior motive, seeking neither to possess nor to enslave them. And if we feel like addressing this sort of child as "prince" or "princess," that is because when we're with them we sense an invitation to take our place as guests at the table of the eternal king in an invisible kingdom. Speaking of the honor and peculiar vocation of our existence, Jesus says:

"The kingdom of heaven may be compared to a king who gave a marriage feast for his son" (Mt. 22:2).

Viewed against this background, Saint-Exupéry's *Little Prince* picks up crucial motifs from the world of the religious imagination. Without the symbolic and spiritual background of Christianity, the Little Prince would never have existed — would not even have been conceivable. Yet he lives only as the fleeting shadow of a once powerful religious light. And the sadness and melancholy, the realm of sunsets and loneliness, that surround him, read like an obituary for something that by rights *ought* to exist, but is only a schematic presence. The book may strike readers as romantically dreamy, the great religious truths may resonate powerfully in it, and we may respond sympathetically to its critique of the adult world, with its superstitious faith in numbers and externalities. But at bottom this splendid literary work, this loveliest of twentieth-century fairy tales, furnishes involuntary proof of how unreachably far we seem to be from the time when dreaming still helped and fairy tales could come true.

This is a story that begins with a description of all the things that grown-ups can destroy in a child before its life has really begun. *The Little Prince,* which claims to be dedicated to an adult (Léon Werth), is really meant for the child that that adult once was. The book conjures all the earth's children not to put their faith in the fancy displays of adults, to hold on to simplicity of heart. But it doesn't show what chance "grown-ups" might stand of changing their evil ways and of finding the way back to their original childhood. Still less does it disclose how the Little Prince might enter his secret kingdom on this earth. On the contrary, in the end the Little Prince returns to his tiny planet out of loyalty to his "rose," while the pilot who has crash-landed proceeds to take up his adult life once again. No doubt he'll do so more sadly and nostalgically than before, but he is nevertheless incapable of assimilating the figure of the Little Prince into his own existence.

Of course, Christianity too reports how, when he comes to this world, the "divine child"[6] is hounded and driven away right from the outset and murdered in the end. Christianity too speaks of waiting for the return of the divine envoy, whose figure we already know and whose message we have heard. But from the religious standpoint the "divine child" is a code name for a fundamentally renewed and redeemed existence. The Little Prince, however, incorporates in an ideal type the longings of an unlived life. He is merely the counter-cipher to the inhuman world of "grown-ups." While religion tells of a dream that has become reality, Saint-Exupéry tells of a dream that never was real, and whose realization is nowhere in sight. The "divine child" of religion embodies a dream that has overcome death, while the Little Prince embodies a childlike existence that was never allowed to come to life. The life that lives in him is not risen but thoroughly stifled. He embodies what was meant to be human nature, what humans' vocation would be if the frost from outside didn't fall all too soon on the first blooms of spring.

A biographical note from *Wind, Sand, and Stars,* in which Saint-Exupéry first uses the image of the "little princes in the fairy tale," will clarify better than any commentary the sense of this coded language. This is the final scene, where Saint-Exupéry is in his railway compartment, wondering about his fellow passengers:

"I sat down face to face with one couple. Between the man and the woman a child had hollowed himself out a place and fallen asleep. He turned in his slumber, and in the dim lamplight I saw his face. What an adorable face! A golden fruit had been born of these two peasants. Forth from these coarse, heavy rags had sprung this miracle of delight and grace.

"I bent over the smooth brow, over those mildly pouting lips, and I said to myself: This is a musician's face. This is the child Mozart. Little princes in legends are no different from this. Protected, sheltered, cultivated, what could this child not become?

"When by mutation a new rose is born in a garden, all the gardeners rejoice. They isolate the rose, tend it, foster it. But there is no gardener for human beings. This little Mozart will be shaped like the rest by the common stamping machine. This little Mozart will love shoddy music in the stench of night dives. This little Mozart is condemned.

"I went back to the sleeping car. I said to myself: Their fate causes these people no suffering. It is not an impulse to charity that has upset me like this. I am not weeping over an eternally open wound. Those who bear the wound do not feel it. It is the human race and not the individual that is wounded here, is outraged here. I do not believe in pity. What torments me here tonight is the gardener's point of view. What torments me is not the poverty to which after all people can accustom themselves as easily as to sloth. Generations of Orientals live in filth and love it. What torments me is not the humps nor the hollows nor the ugliness. It is the sight, a little bit in all these people, of Mozart murdered."[7]

The Little Prince is a "murdered Mozart," a nostalgic memory of, and a mournful hope in, a life that would have been called to greatness, if people would only let it. But they have dulled and deadened it in the bud by replacing all the mind's alertness and sensitivity with a terror-stricken stultification through the organized annihilation of the emotions. In place of artistic productivity, the reality of dream and fantasy, they have put the trash of entertainment and the flatness of mass consumption. They have replaced harmonics, listening to the music of the spheres and the universe, with electronic pounding. They have replaced literature, poetry, tenderness, and love with verbal cascades of cynicism and the freezing of emotion with logic and linguistic dissection. They have replaced painting, gazing at the natural forms hidden in the things of this world, with the huckstering prostitution and deformation of beauty. They have replaced prayer, the silent experience of the holy, with the marketing of all our words, the systematic destruction of the soul. No longer do the musician, the poet, the painter, and the priest serve as fundamental figures of the human capacity to perceive and express the truth. No, even Saint-Exupéry's Little Prince doesn't show us how we might live as "grown-ups"; he simply bemoans the fact that we turned into "grown-ups" to begin with. The Fall has taken place, and the path back to Paradise is nowhere to be seen. On the other hand, we have already gained a great deal if we have become capable of feeling a certain melancholy, if we've started to rediscover something that lies deep within us and begs to be admitted to life. The Little Prince should be understood as a psychic image of something in us that was killed before it managed to live, as an evocative code name for what has been lost, as an eternal portrait of something that has gone unlived and yet absolutely demands to be lived.

But then who are Mozart's murderers? Who are these Philistine soul-killers and stranglers of humanity? The answer can only be the people whom we ourselves generally consider "adults," the people who have set their lives up in a state where emotional frigidity, cynicism, and hope-lessness are the norm. We admire them because they've succeeded in giving up hoping and waiting for anything. In the middle of life they have died, because they are lit-erally "finished," and they finish off everything that is not, like them, "grown up."

Chapter 2

The Grown-ups:
Portraits of Loneliness

CB

IMAGINE IF WE FOLLOWED the footsteps of the Little Prince, as if we literally came from a strange star and could see with the relentlessly honest eyes of a child. As we approach the world that we find familiar and ordinary to the point of nausea, it reveals itself to be a waxworks of vanity, futility, and complete incapacity to love anything outside itself. It looks like a bewildering gallery of cranky eccentrics, all inhabiting their own private planets. They seem to be light years removed from all human beings, as they are from all human behavior. They are creatures who take themselves to be "serious people," merely because they turn everything into numbers, while they themselves are only "sponges," sucking everything up without inwardly transforming it, just to make themselves "weighty" and "big" in the eyes of others.[1]

Thus the first thing we meet on the Little Prince's planetary voyage is the sad spectacle of the lonely, senile "king." He can view all men and women only as his subjects, and he thinks his commands can shape whatever happens. The space occupied by his world, which is completely covered by the ermine of his robe, is minuscule, but he hasn't even made a serious attempt to get to know this little world of his. Supposedly an absolute monarch, whose will seems to rule over everything around him, he doesn't have the least notion of the real world.[2] His dealings with people are limited to the question of how to insert them into, and exploit them once they're inside, the framework of his fictitious power interests. Meanwhile it becomes immediately evident that the principles of what Kant would call his "practical reason" are completely abstract and alien to humanity. Still, this king has learned that authority must be supported by reason, and so he can issue commands only when they are compatible with the course of nature. To that extent we might consider him a lot kinder and wiser than most of the "big shots" of this world, who have likewise gone prematurely senile and gotten ossified in their power. Indeed, if invited to meet one of the latter, you might bring along a copy of *The Little Prince* and quote to him a remark made by the king: "If I ordered a general to fly from one flower to another like a butterfly, or to write a tragic drama, and if the general did not carry out the order that he had received"[3] – then it wouldn't be the general's fault.

There's no point in trying to transmogrify Philistines and pragmatists into poets and heaven-stormers – we can only agree with the king's wisdom here. Nevertheless this sort of unnatural ordering still goes on, inevitably amid the pomp and circumstance of a solemnly boring etiquette, in the raiment of godlike directives, and with an insistence on slavish obedience. But, cruel as it may be to order generals to float like butterflies, it strikes us as much worse to take people with the sensibility, tenderness, and beauty of butterflies and force them to line themselves and others up in rigid rank and file. This is exactly what the king tries to do with the Little Prince. He claims to have grasped the fact that you can command only when you yourself are capable of obedience. But in fact he never renounces his imaginary omnipotence, and hence he never lets things flow with their natural rhythm. On the contrary, he insists on appointing the Little Prince to the alien office of judge, simply to condemn the old rat on his planet to death. So even where the king proclaims so-called wisdom, he babbles self-serving, wrong-headed phrases that simply aim at enlarging his halo and concealing his objective impotence. In truth the man, who poses as so gentle and understanding, is a cruel despot who loves to terrorize others so that they'll spend their entire lives dependent on his "grace."

It's typical of such senile monarchs that they always have to be judging, condemning, and sentencing people; and they won't accept correction. The armor of their prejudices is impenetrable. Thus the Little Prince has basically nothing to say to the constantly commanding king. One of the sad points made by this fairy tale is that nowhere in the story do we get even a hint of how the "big shots" might possibly undergo a positive transformation. Their incapacity for dialogue, their spiritual isolation, their narcissistic ghettoes know no bounds. It's a priori senseless to talk to them, and even if you break off contact with them, they'll interpret that as a triumph of their towering importance. When the Little Prince takes his leave of the king, feeling bored, irritated, and disgusted, he hears the monarch appointing him his ambassador. But what kind of reports could he file, except to say that this kind of life isn't worthwhile, is hardly suited to promoting a person's happiness? "If any one would be first, he must be last of all and servant of all" (Mk. 9:35) would be the only message that from the "children's" perspective would be worth bringing to the world from the king's planet. But this message would mean the end of all "kings," and in *The Little Prince* there's no hope of that. You can pass over the "kings," but you can't change them.

Still, some people are even worse than that. The "kings" want to be recognized for the rank they hold and the role they play. They're proud of their office, and their office makes them proud. Still harder to bear are the conceited fools who have the nerve to stand there ostentatiously as if their mere existence made them more distinguished than all other mortals. With their lust for fawning admirers they automatically condemn themselves to a world of unyielding isolation. It's impossible to live for any length of time with people who always have one and the same question on their lips: How will you praise my appearance? Raise my prestige? Extol my intelligence, honor my views, and abase yourself in every way so as to mirror my complaisant self-image? The real "big shots" can only tolerate being the greatest, and the only way they encounter other people is by strutting and pluming themselves in front of them, hoping to be rated as (at least somewhat) superior, more handsome and intelligent than the rest. Thus for the "big shots" every meeting with others turns into a ruthless competition for the favor of their fellows. But, paradoxically enough, though you may be amused by their narcissistic moods and their addiction to applause, you quickly begin to notice the wretched monotonousness, the unbearable egocentricity, the complete lack of interest in other people's fate that marks the "vain person."

And from this moment on you'll have the hardest time feeding them what they're hungriest for: respect, appreciation, and recognition.

As surely as the domineering and megalomaniacal king has to acknowledge his complete powerlessness, so the vain types, despite their yearning for recognition and admiration, are destined to reap nothing but rejection and contempt. But they'll learn as little from this experience as the king did. With every frustration they'll be all the more breathlessly insistent on soliciting praise for their uniqueness. And they'll continually find that with their competitive mentality, their insincerity and superficiality, they're all the more certain of provoking other people to hostility and secret revenge. "Therefore," says Jesus in the Sermon on the Mount, "do not be anxious, saying, 'What shall we eat?' or 'What shall we drink?' or 'What shall we wear?' For the Gentiles seek all these things" (Mt. 6:31–32). He is suggesting that every one could possess an inalienable beauty, beyond that of the sparrows and lilies, and that our value doesn't depend on the elegance of our ties or dresses. But who among the "big shots" will heed this simple message of "children"?

Anyhow, the vain person keeps looking, however futilely, for some sort of human relationship. We can take a further step up the scale of unfulfilled lust for life, lonely egocentrism, and sad excess, and then we arrive at the planet of the "tippler." He is, we might say, broken-down vanity, a man who can no longer stand looking himself in the eye. Instead of working on themselves and seeking out the roots of their self-hatred, such individuals prefer personal oblivion. There is a certain level of self-contempt at which one feels something almost like a duty to make oneself as vile as possible.[4] Disappointment at the impossibility of achieving their peculiar greatness compels some people to despair out of weakness[5] and leads to the desperate attempt to pickle themselves forever in melancholic self-pity.[6] There's nothing more to hope from others — how could they have compassion on such a wretched weakling, on a person who has lost himself and given up?[7] And so the addicts cling to some dead object as a fetish, as if it had the power to restore lost life or at least to offer protection from the glances of other people and, most of all, from their own wretchedness.[8] This quickly creates a vicious circle, and what was supposed to be a remedy for self-contempt gradually turns into the main cause of increasing dependency, deception, and debasement. Human contact is replaced by auto-intoxication. And the moments of oblivion designed to choke off the feeling of self-revulsion actually serve to aggravate the burden of wretchedness to the point that it becomes unbearable. It can often happen that others, like the Little Prince, will be moved to pity at the sight of this kind of self-enslavement. But how is one to help people who shun all dialogue, all explanations, all exertion, while their behavior becomes increasingly infantile, and ultimately all they want is to be left in peace?

In the end the life of such a person is reminiscent of the man in the Gospel who buried his "talent" out of sheer terror at having to render an account of it, and finally has nothing at all to show for his wasted life (Mt. 25:24–30).

Meanwhile, along with this trio of negative self-pleasurers, there are three more planets, inhabited by characters who plunge into the world — where they infallibly come to grief. Actually in their own way they all want to reach lonely greatness, but in fact the only great thing about them is their loneliness, and the only amazing thing about them is their failure to grasp what true greatness is. The self-destruction of the *alcoholic* can represent the attempt to inhale the entire world, simply to do in his mind. The reverse form of this addiction is *greed*, the seemingly sharp-witted but actually absurd transformation of the whole world into an office building–warehouse, possibly culminating in the ruin of the planet.[9]

Perhaps at this point, where the basic issue is the relationship of the "big shots" to nature, we have to listen to the voices of some "children of nature," in order to understand the cultural critique implied in *The Little Prince* vis-à-vis the world where the mantras are "business," "profit," and "marketing." "It's a repugnant kind of arrogance on the part of the white man," explains the Sioux shaman, Tahca Ushte, "to put himself over God and to say: 'I'll let this animal live, because it makes money.' Or, 'This animal has to go, it doesn't pay; the space it takes up can be put to more profitable use.' "[10] "For the white man every blade of grass and every waterhole has a price tag on it."[11] "And the prairie is gradually becoming a lifeless landscape – no more prairie dogs, no badgers, no foxes, no coyotes. The great birds of prey, of course, fed on the prairie dogs. Nowadays it's a rare day that you see an eagle. The bald eagle is the symbol of this country. You see them on your money, but it's your money that's killing them. Once a nation begins to destroy its own symbol, then it's not exactly on the best path."[12]

In the same vein the Indian Tatanga Mani argues: "There are many foolish things about your so-called civilization. You white men run after money like lunatics until you have so much of it that you can't live long enough to spend it. You plunder the forests, the soil, you squander the natural fuels, as if another generation weren't coming after you that would need all this as much as you do."[13]

Apart from the "ecological" accent, which was by no means alien to Saint-Exupéry,[14] though not directly mentioned in *The Little Prince,* this critique of our culture by the "children of nature" comes down to the same point. *The Little Prince* likewise finds one feature of the "big people" totally insane: their compulsion to transform everything into hot investments and cold cash.

The value of money, we might say, lies in its being a universal means of exchange. And this rather abstract quality readily leads to the superstition that money can buy anything your mind conceives or your heart desires. All too easily people fail to realize that the really desirable things are not for sale. As Saint-Exupéry says, the crucial thing here is the mental "nexus" between things. Friends, for example, can't be gotten in a store.[15] The danger of money is that it may turn from a means of exchange for all possible goods into the quintessence of all possible values, into a metaphysical entity. In that case dealing with money no longer means enjoying the things that money *can,* after all, buy. The idea is now to get as much money as possible, not to buy, but to be able to buy.

This is exactly how we define people of money, the capitalists, who renounce all private enjoyment of money so they can have a lot of it and make a whole lot more. To these people, if they are "grown-ups," nothing will seem unattainable. They have the habit of using money to transform everything into property: mountains, lakes, forests, deserts and shores, steppes and seas – everything, along with countless species of plants and animals, will all belong to those who can pay the highest price for them. And once again they will have to pay the exact amount that can presumably be earned, on average, from the sale of such "stuff."[16] As a matter of fact, why not start selling the moon and the stars? You just have to be energetic and quick enough to steal a march on your potential competitors. Not only is all the space in the universe for sale, but time itself is money. And the more money sets its seal on life and swallows it up, the more it takes on the character of a living thing. If getting a lot of money is the best way to make still more money, then the logic of money achieves its real triumph when we realize that money can't buy anything more precious than — money. We have to learn that the possibilities of using money to earn more money are the true value of money.

At this moment the genius of the "businessman" breathes a soul into money: Once and for all it ceases to have a certain meaning as a means of exchange. From now on it dominates all human dealings as the sole meaningful source. It multiplies in the banks, it rules in the parliaments, it designates emperors, popes, and kings. It is infinitely mightier than the mighty; it has every possible quality. The Little Prince thinks that the power of money to animate everything and to confer omnipotence is "almost poetic." But we're talking about the fantasy of maniacs, the hallucination of a nightmare, something we'd dismiss as unreal if it didn't have the power to assert itself everywhere as *the* reality. In his addiction to alcohol the "tippler" wants to descend into intoxication to forget himself and the world, but he winds up simply destroying himself. The greedy man, on the other hand, transforms the whole world into an addictive intoxicant, laying waste to everything: "For what does it profit a man, to gain the whole world and forfeit his life?" (Mk. 8:36). People willing and able to buy everything with money must first have sold themselves, body and soul, to money, and then the richer they get the poorer they are.[17] They are, in the deepest sense of the term, useless, utter and complete parasites whose narcissistic egocentricity is incapable of dialogue or insight. To this type as well the Little Prince has nothing to say. To the "businessman" the Little Prince means nothing more than a waste of time, so the Little Prince takes the first opportunity to make himself scarce.

One common feature of all the "grown-up" planet-dwellers we have seen so far is that they were chasing, as if hypnotized, after goals that, however absurd and senseless they might be, were subjectively prompted by self-interest. But the Little Prince is not spared the grotesque spectacle of the "big shots' " power to turn even duty and loyalty into egocentric folly.

The example par excellence of this is furnished on the fifth planet by the *lamplighter,* a man who, like all his predecessors on the path of this sheer travesty of what it means to be human, has neither a personal name nor a personal face. All he has is an occupational label, a job description, into which his whole existence seamlessly blends. He is a person who if asked, "Who are you?" would have to say, "I'm employed." For this man doesn't care what sense or purpose his work has. The only thing that counts for him are the rules he has to follow, regardless of what they say. The time has long since passed when the instructions for lamplighting could still fit into the real course of things. Meanwhile this man's little planet spins on and on far more rapidly. But what full-fledged functionaries or traditionalists would be fazed by the fact that their job description, i.e. in this case literally their worldview, is hopelessly passé? Instead of stopping to reflect and risking self-correction, this sort of "on-duty" person will always run, puffing and panting for breath, after the accelerat-

ing spin of the world. Because on call is on call, rules are
rules, you have to do your duty, and the early bird catches
the worm.

There can be only one redemption from this hellish
duty, and the Little Prince tries to suggest it: The lamplighter has to let himself, just once, follow the path of the
sun "privately," and then dream about the beauty of sunsets. Beyond "work time" the lamplighter has to rediscover
"life time";[18] his planet is small enough for that. But it's all
in vain. The life of this "slave to duty" is split into occupational drudgery and the futile wish for "rest," in the sense
of sleep, switching-off, extinction. And this man will do
his job ever more hectically and exhaustedly. He too is an
addict, as unteachable and incapable of change as all the
other "big people," and above all unable to harmonize his
will with his actions, or vice versa. Though he does his
job so faithfully, he actually curses it. His work is not his
chosen vocation; he bemoans what he has to do, and he be-
wails his fate. His reading of himself and the world is that
he is and will forever remain a victim of the circumstances
that prescribe what's to be done. For all his busyness his
own mystery remains hidden to him. He's unaware that
amid all the hustle and bustle of his work he is in fact a man
without a will, a lazy shirker who never finds rest precisely
because that's *all* he wants. If he could bring his desires
and plans into his work, the job would immediately find
its proper measure, its goal and its limit. It would be part
of an existence that was lived and fulfilled from within.
But, as it is, it remains a burdensome task, a never-ending,
sheerly incomprehensible, restless grind. Here too there's
no escaping the vicious circle. And on this cramped little planet of dutifulness and lethargy, of overexertion and
spiritual idleness, it's impossible to realize any form what-

soever of community, exchange, or life as a member of a couple.

We should note that what the lamplighter has to do could in itself be a highly romantic and poetic activity, a world full of melancholy dreams and gentle "sunsets." But the way the lamplighter "performs" or "discharges" his office allows no one to come near him. His work warps itself into wearisome monotony, tiresome complaints, and miserable monologues. "Look at the birds of the air: they neither reap nor sow nor gather into barns.... Therefore do not be anxious" (Mt. 26:31). We might like to remind all the "lamplighters" of this verse, but they would surely come up with immediate proof that in their kind of service such teachings can't be "implemented" and in any event run contrary to official regulations.

Nevertheless the lamplighter's workaholism is sharply distinct from the obsessions that haunt the tippler or the other-directed vain man[19] on the second planet. Still, objectively speaking, his activity, as a service, has a certain spiritual dimension. And even if the man himself does his utmost to get through it as mindlessly and joylessly as possible, it is enveloped by a certain gleam of commitment, responsibility, and courage, which are thoroughly spiritual. Meanwhile the people who want to be really "great" ultimately succeed in transforming the freest thing of all, the mind, into an unreal, empty, illusory life, into pedantic showing-off, a hodge-podge of highfalutin terms. Their language points to nothing except a conceited claim to encyclopedic omniscience and universal *savoir vivre* – a presumptuous pseudo-kingdom, even more fantastic than the megalomania of the commanding king.

The last type of such (non-)human beings is the *geographer*. He has the perfect look of the bookworm, the

ink-stained theoretician, and the solemnly berobed emi-
nence, because in a remarkable way he has witnessed a
split between the world of thought and the world of experience, between the level of "logic," as Saint-Exupéry likes
to call it, and the level of existence, between the weight
of science and the rightness of knowledge. He rates the
outside world and real life as a useless waste of time, mere
idle running around. Learning *about* life strikes him as
incomparably more estimable than living experience itself. He's too good for such experience, since his abilities
are oriented toward passing judgment on other people's
experiences. Seeing himself, examining himself, experiencing himself doesn't agree with the lifestyle of such a
busy, hard-working "scientist." In a posture of noble intellectual distance he prefers or demands simply to cultivate
the art of delivering verdicts. He knows the moral value
of a person. *He* decides what is valid and invalid. *He* gives
directions about what is and isn't worth knowing. Without realizing it, he is condemned by this mania for passing
judgment, this reduction of experience to merely taking
cognizance of reports about other people's experience,
to an insatiable hunger for reality. But meanwhile that
longing proves incapable of penetrating the ghetto of his
methodical discretion. His parasitical vicarious life claims
to be celebrating itself as knowledge of what is permanent,
but his quasi-metaphysical abstinence vis-à-vis the imper-
manent prevents him from discovering anything living as
real. Adventures and risk taking are the furthest thing from
his mind. He couldn't even imagine that truth grows only
where somebody dares to broadcast his own or her own
life as its seed.

We must clearly see the difference here.

On his search for a passage across South America, Magellan was forced to recognize that the enormous outlet of the Rio de la Plata was just the mouth of a river.[20] He then dared to make the icy passage around Tierra del Fuego. He set sail into an unknown ocean, enduring a time when supplies on board had run so low that he and his men had either to sail back to South America or continue, for better or worse, on what they surmised was the route to India. He sailed out into the most enormous watery wilderness in the world, amid tormenting calm, in hope that had no prospects. This is what discoverers and searchers do. The "professor," by contrast, catalogues and maps somebody else's knowledge while sitting in an ivory tower.

It was Søren Kierkegaard who fought against this, especially in the field of "theology." He angrily attacked the transformation of discourse about God into theories about God, of experiencing God into teaching "divinity," which he exposed as a cheat. He asked how in heaven anyone could lead a life of wealth, status, and popularity gained by preaching the "message of salvation" of how Jesus was poor, despised, and murdered.[21] On a similar note Friedrich Nietzsche ironically called historians even greater men than Alexander the Great, because while Alexander merely made history by fighting the battle of Gaugamela, the professor of history added to those deeds the knowledge of what they meant.[22] And we could continue in this vein: The great poets, painters, and musicians have often lived on the verge of starvation or madness, with shattered nerves, distraught by their contemporaries' lack of understanding. But once they're safely in their graves some Ph.D. candidate or assistant professor will show up to build his or her career and live quite comfortably by demonstrating how great Baudelaire, Tchaikovsky, or Van Gogh "really" were.

For this sort of perverse intellectual it's enough to preach a "faith" without "works," to proclaim a worldview without experiencing the world, and to build an entire existence quite literally on "sand" (Mt. 7:26). The original reports of discoverers and circumnavigators are used to set up a rootless "bazaar of ideas,"[23] where people dicker only about the market value of phrases; and the place of origin of an artistically knotted "carpet" simply determines the price that the idea salesperson hopes to get.

The "geographers" are basically "businesspeople." They too are "addicts," "vain," "lamplighters of fashion," as well as "kings" of madness. And the more you try to show them what real life is, with its poetry, devotion, and love, they'll rate it as petty and all too trivial for their eager attention. It all makes you want to praise God for the truths that God has hidden from the "great and wise," in order to make them known to the "little ones" (Mt. 11:5).

This concludes the Little Prince's sky journey, his panoramic survey, and it leaves behind the impression of an amused sadness. There's no doubt about it: All the "big people" are so grotesque, so bizarre, so isolated, and it's worthwhile to borrow the honest eyes of a child and expose the negative poetry of their existence in all its wretchedness. If that's how the "adults" are, then it's better to be and remain a "child."

But who will redeem the "great ones" from their "greatness," and how? That's the crucial question. If we believe the Little Prince, there's really no way to help the "big people," and the reason for this impossibility is the reason for the distress they're trapped in. Their loneliness, their isolation, their self-centeredness, their fantastic capacity to pursue happiness in life as if they were possessed (in a way guaranteed to make them unhappy), their permanent monologue and monomania, their complete inability to listen to, or even learn from, another person — all this obviously makes it impossible to humanize the "big shots." We need to do more than draw a grimly accurate and horrible picture of the compulsions and vicious circles that mark the physiognomy of "grown-ups." The decisive thing is to understand the root causes why the "big shots" find themselves forced into the monstrous conditions of their existence. For example:

• People like the king, living on their lonely planets, would have to work through their fear of impotence, insignificance, and pure meaninglessness. Only then could a love strong enough to restore their faith in the true value of their life come and liberate them from their arrogantly usurped thrones.

• In the behavior of the vain man we have to recognize the cruel torment of his despair, his inability to acknowledge himself, his deadly fear of disrespect and contempt. And only when his own eyes become a mirror enabling him to rediscover the radiance of his own beauty will his quest for applause from other people come to an end.

• We have to understand that the tippler's spineless lust for oblivion and self-extinction contains a desperate longing to do something to break down the exaggerated claims he's making on himself. Only then will he have enough self-confidence to lend him a certain solidity and fidelity to himself, thus breaking the links in the suicidal chain of unavoidable frustration.

• We have to realize that the businessman is suffering from chronic fear of the void, of miserable poverty, of helplessness in the face of the constant possible challenges to his external existence. Only then can hope remove his fear of death. Such a hope could make his inner life mature so richly and fully that the greed for material possessions would become pointless.

• We have to sense how the lamplighter is driven by the fear of being totally wrong and unjustified the moment he takes a step away from the dictates of others. Only then can we get him to give up his fear of freedom, his fear of chaos, and flight from himself in exchange for a deeper affirmation and the decision to live his own life and take on his own responsibilities. Then even his duty-racked existence could find rest in a freely chosen balance between obligation and inclination.

• Last of all, we have to recognize in the portrait of the geographer the fear of reality, of the depth of feeling, the height of enthusiasm, the breadth of longing, and above all the fear he has of everything that won't stand still, everything uncertain and transitory. Only then can he be shown that the unchanging and the eternal are reflected in the apparently trivial and fleeting moments of our everyday routine. Then even this sort of person can be taught the art of life, and not just the news about it.[24]

All these martyrs of the ego have to rediscover and radiate within themselves a bit of their lost childhood, of trust in their hidden kingdom, a piece of the Little Prince himself. And the Little Prince will have to sniff out the place where, amid types that first strike him as so alien, he can once again find himself. That's the only way to forge a healing alliance between the "big people" and the "Little Prince." Otherwise we'll get no further than a regretful shake of the head over the vices and distortions of "grown-ups," instead of having a real encounter, a process where the "big shots" can experience a fruitful purgation.

But this is precisely a subject that Saint-Exupéry never mentions. Though he demanded and praised commitment, dedication, and self-sacrifice for a great common cause, he obviously could see the "big people" only as lost souls, instead of a task to be worked on. As if they didn't have enough troubles of their own already. Saint-Exupéry's Little Prince is content to find these unfortunate creatures "strange" and then turn his back on them. So what we get is contempt instead of hope, resignation instead of effort, failure instead of redemption — and not by chance. I have argued that *The Little Prince* fails to embody the religious figure of a reborn existence brought back to life, but only condenses a sort of melancholy reminiscence of something lost all too early on. If this is true, then the book's typology of "grown-ups" turns out to be stiff and unchangeable. It never gives a hint of how any kind of mediation or integration of its polar opposites might be achieved.

As we look at this world of "grown-ups," is there simply nothing to do, nothing to hope for, nothing more to expect? Well, thank God, that's not the way it is. There is something like a teaching of the desert, and for Saint-Exupéry these lessons in privation ultimately prove to be something like hope after all, a hope by dint of despair.

Chapter 3

The Wisdom of the Desert
and the Quest of Love

CB

T HE EARTH, which the Little Prince visits on his planetary journey, is overflowing with "grown-ups," but at the same time, or rather precisely because of this, it's a "desert," a place of loneliness,[1] of salt-encrusted mountains,[2] washed by the echoing waves of human voices that degenerate into the monotonous roar of solitude.[3] This is no place for life; it's a valley of death. In Saint-Exupéry's language "desert" means above all the "human desert." It's not a point in space, but a state of meaninglessness, of spiritual desiccation, an accumulation of nothing and nothings. One need only read Saint-Exupéry's famous "Letter to General X" to comprehend this stifling in external things, this oozing away of the soul, this bogging down of every stirring of the heart as the central problem of all his creative life, his sadness, and his torment. Let me cite a few passages from it:

"Today I'm profoundly sad — it goes very deep. I'm sad for my generation, which has been emptied of all human substance. The only form of spiritual life it's gotten to know is bars, mathematics, and Bugatti racing cars; and it finds itself today in what is strictly a herd action – an action that no longer has any kind of color. Nobody even notices it anymore."[4]

"I hate my epoch with all my soul. Man is dying of thirst in it. Ah, General, there is only one problem, one single problem in the world. How can we restore to people some spiritual meaning, some spiritual unrest; how to make something like a Gregorian chant rain down on them? If I were a believer, there'd be no doubt that once this time of the 'necessary, thankless job' is over, the only place I could bear would be Solesmes. Look, people can no longer live on refrigerators and politics, on balance sheets and crossword puzzles. They can't do it anymore. . . . Two billion men and women are just listening to the robot. All they can understand is the robot, and one day they'll turn into robots themselves."[5]

"The bonds of love that link today's men and women to creatures and things are so slack, so thin, that their absence isn't as noticeable as before. . . . The refrigerators are interchangeable; the houses too, if they're merely an assemblage. And woman? And religion? And the party? You can't even be unfaithful anymore. Whom could you be unfaithful to? . . . *The human desert.*"[6]

"People today are kept in line, depending on the milieu, by skat or bridge. We have been astonishingly well castrated. So now we're finally free. Our arms and legs have been cut off, then they let us walk around. But I hate this epoch, where people become, under a universal totalitarianism, gentle, polite, and peaceful cattle. We're supposed to take this as moral progress. What I hate about Marxism is the totalitarianism it leads to. It defines the individual as a producer and consumer: The crucial problem is distribution. That's how it is on the model farms. What I hate about Nazism is the totalitarianism that it strives for by its very essence...the truth of the people!...What will become of...us...in this epoch...of the robot-man, the termite-man, the man who swings back and forth between assembly-line work on the Bedeau system and playing skat? People have been castrated of all their creative energy, and down in their villages they can't even create a dance or song anymore. People are supplied with ready-made culture, with standard culture, the way cows are provided with hay. That's what they look like – the people of today."[7]

As can be seen in another passage, Saint-Exupéry knows all about the social background of this deracination through a stifling delight in consumption. He sees and laments the destruction of tradition, the divergence of science and human nature, of knowledge and education. And he continually and insistently points to and calls for the replacement of all the destroyed values by the mass chucking of commodities, which by their very excess rob themselves of their intrinsic value. "There are two hundred million men in Europe whose existence has no meaning and who yearn to come alive. Industry has torn them from the idiom of their peasant lineage and has locked them up in those enormous ghettoes that are like railway yards heaped with blackened trucks. Out of the depths of their slums these men yearn to be awakened. There are others, caught in the wheels of a thousand trades, who are forbidden to share in the joys known to a Mermoz, to a priest, to a man of science. Once it was believed that to bring these creatures to manhood it was enough to feed them, clothe them, and look to their everyday needs; but we see now that the result of this has been to turn out petty shop-keepers, village politicians, hollow technicians devoid of an inner life. Some indeed were well taught, but no one troubled to cultivate any of them. People who believe that culture consists in the capacity to remember formulae have a paltry notion of what it is. Of course any science student can tell us more about nature and her laws than Descartes or Newton — but what can he tell us about the human spirit? With more or less awareness, all men feel the need to come alive."[8]

In these vehement and impotently longing complaints we keep coming back to the religious code of the renewal of life, of the "child," of the new beginning. And for Saint-Exupéry this yearning takes on its purest form right in the middle of the "desert." The "desert" is not simply just the place of "tohu-wa-bohu," of chaos and confusion, of privation and perversion. It's also an inexorable proving ground, where the truth comes out, the place of the prophet and people seeking God,[9] the smelting furnace of mystical transformation, a locus of loneliness and truthfulness, literally the "garden of Allah," as the Arabs call the Sahara. When Saint-Exupéry speaks of the desert, he naturally has in mind his own real experiences in the deserts of North Africa. He has exact knowledge about the mysterious power with which the desert shapes men and women, melting off all superfluity, attachments, and fat, strafing them quite literally with a sandblaster.

To understand the formative force of the desert, you have to witness something like the salt caravans that come out of the interior of Chad, crossing thousands of kilometers on their way. These people reckon their age not in years but by the number of caravans they've taken part in — twenty caravan trips are a very advanced age. Were they to report of the hardships met with on their journeys, they'd tell most of all about the willpower they have to muster to cover a specific distance day after day, struggling against sand, wind, thirst, and exhaustion, to get to a certain water tank. They'd tell of the shimmering heat by day and the biting cold by night, the feeling of being tiny and powerless amid the boundless distance. Overhead is the blue-gray dome of the heavens or the glittering band of stars and all around them no other sound than the howling of the khamsin and the snorting of the camels. The men and women of the desert know how completely they are at the mercy of nature's powers, as if the landscape itself wanted to teach them the attitude of submission to God (Islam).[10]

But precisely here, amid the trials and renunciation, every drop of water and every breath of life – because you have to stake your whole life on them – are precious beyond all measure. The desert itself teaches you a fresh appreciation of the value of things. And actually this is the only hope that Saint-Exupéry appears to have left in the face of the desolate landscape of the human world: "The men in the desert or the monastery, who possess nothing, see clearly where their joys come from, and so they preserve more easily the very source of their fervor."[11]

So everything seems to depend on making people feel the "desert" of their lives as intensely as possible, until the energy of longing awakes to relieve in them the stifling weight of overconsumption and the "fatty degeneration" of the heart. Then going to the well is more important than drinking, because the privations one endures lend the well in the desert its mystery and its beauty. Saint-Exupéry is sure that not only do people want to know what to live on, but that, far more important, they absolutely have to know what they're here for. And this goal that gives their life meaning is never a thing, but the meaning that ties the things together — something invisible, to be seen only with the "eyes of the heart," as Saint-Exupéry points out in connection with a verse from the Bible (Eph. 1:18). For this very reason, Saint-Exupéry looks at the desert as a place of healing and salvation, as it is in Old Testament prophecy. Only there can you experience the holy; only there can you meet the Little Prince.

That explains why the Little Prince, before he enters the desert, that redemptive counter-world to the ostensible consumer paradise and that scene of a possible transformation, first meets the serpent of death. As in Christian symbolism the way to truth is compared with dying, or a descent into the underworld.[12] Thus, anyone who visits the desert must learn to accept death, the limitedness of existence, the finiteness of earthly life in both its anxious and comforting inevitability.

If we are to move beyond the illusory world of "grown-ups," with their superficiality, their nervous, hectic rush, and their frantic destruction of all values, we need above all a clear look at the kindly-cruel destiny of death, the inescapable poison of the snake on the sandy floor of the desert. It is as if the whole hustle and bustle of the "grown-up" world was designed simply to anesthetize the fear of death. But all their efforts finally boil down to ceasing to mourn for anything, since nothing has any value anymore. There is nothing permanent on the surface of things; there is nothing that would deserve a tribute of grief for its transitoriness. Hence if everything is transformed into the superficial, there is nothing left for which the pain of mourning would "pay." In truth, however, the serpent of death can teach us something quite different, a deeper lesson: In a world of mortality nothing can be taken for granted. The more clearly it appears how unnecessary any one existence is, the more everything regains its surprising density, its baffling uniqueness.

Everything that is and happens deserves the greatest attentiveness, precisely in the face of death. And, conversely, the delusory arrogance and conceit of power, possessions, and knowledge dwindle away when all things are mortal. Death relativizes the things we presume to cling to, as if they guaranteed our security. It bestows a calm wisdom, even an ultimate peace: When the burden of the earth becomes too heavy, there are always the gates of death, the mysterious omnipotence of the serpent, who is always ready to solve the puzzle of the mind and to heal the body's pains.[13] People who see the snake inevitably look into the depths of things; right before their eyes they find life taking on a new shape.

In many fairy tales the hero goes off in search of ultimate reality on the frontier zones between Outside and Inside, between the Surface and the Depths, between Here and Beyond. On this quest he is met by animal helpers who speak to him and show him the way into the counterworld of his consciousness. In *The Little Prince* this is the role played by the "fox," who also makes frequent appearances in *Grimms' Fairy Tales*, for example, in "The Golden Bird."[14] The fox has a long pedigree in the history of religion, because he is evidently a European descendant of the jackal-headed Egyptian god Anubis, the faithful companion of the mourning Isis as she wanders in search of her beloved brother and husband, Osiris, who was dismembered and whose limbs were scattered over the Nile delta.[15] The mystery of Anubis lies in his magical knowledge of how to bring the dead back to life, and this same function apparently also belongs to the fox in *The Little Prince*, because on the border to the land beyond the desert his advice is literally life-saving.

The Little Prince has barely stepped onto the earth and approached the human world, when he immediately sees himself faced with an extreme challenge. No one can exist without having something to live for, something he or she considers uniquely beautiful and precious, and for the Little Prince this uniquely precious thing has hitherto been the "rose" on his little planet. Up till now the rose has perforce seemed to him perfectly incomparable, for the sole reason that back there it appeared to be a miracle, and he had never had the opportunity to compare his rose with another one. But now, at the edge of a whole field full of roses, this comparison forces itself upon him with stunning necessity and threatens to make his whole life totter.

Sometimes it happens that a thing we've always had absolute faith in collapses, something that we've previously revered and loved as unique all at once proves to be a mere instance of a species merrily reproducing itself ad infinitum. The thing we have hung our affections on suddenly seems devalued and hollow, thanks to the "inflation" caused by the sheer frequency of its occurrence. Inevitably we feel not just disappointed, but completely orphaned and homeless: We no longer know what to attach our hearts to. This is precisely what the Little Prince feels when he sees before him some five thousand roses. It's a moment when everything is on the line for him: The question of the uniqueness of his rose will decide for him the meaning of the whole world, his joy, his hope, whence he comes and whither he'll go. Everything depends on the Little Prince's understanding where the uniqueness of his rose lies. That uniqueness is not an objective quality, nor an external feature. It derives from a psychic attitude and can be perceived only from within. It is one's own heart that lends the other its value and fills it with meaning. But this is exactly the lesson of the "fox," the content of his magical introduction to the inner world of love.

When all is said and done,the teachings of the fox don't tell the Little Prince anything essentially new. They merely make him aware of the dangers of superficiality. They let him see where his inner wealth lies, what the uniqueness of his rose consists in. He now has to repeat explicitly on a higher plane, and get a solid personal grip on, the things he used to do automatically on his planet. Before this the rose on his planet had struck the Little Prince as an accident, a windfall that suddenly landed in his world. And without noticing it, as he simply strove day in, day out to comply with her wishes and moods, as he admired her beauty and protected her delicate condition, an inner bond of trust and familiarity was forged between him and the rose. It linked them both together naturally, unpremeditatedly. So without realizing it the Little Prince had learned the mystery of friendship, because, as the fox explains, *friendship* consists precisely in the patient, gradually ripening process of familiarizing oneself, of "taming."

In love, as with everything humanly valuable, it is absurd to try to "save" time and harvest the fruit before it blooms and ripens in keeping with the standards of the "grown-up" people. All haste, all pressure, all precipitousness can only do harm to love. Because the shyest and most sensitive lovers, the most longing, the most bashful, the most passionate among them, need the slow movements toward intimacy that will take away their fear of the "hunters" and gradually accustom them to the presence of the other, who will daily become more familiar. You can't buy affection, trust, tenderness, the dream-filled presence of a person you love with all your heart. But step by step you can learn to understand the language of her eyes, the expression of her mouth, and the gestures of her hands. Something infinitely precious, unique, and incomparably valuable begins to communicate itself in all this. You can see the soul of your beloved gleaming through in the hidden signs of her face, you can lift that soul more brightly into the light, illuminating it with every glance from your own eyes. You can gradually learn to understand the meaning of her words, because the words link up together differently in her language than in yours — they point to fields of alien memories. If you follow their hints, they will turn into paths that lead to the heart of the beloved. And the more you learn to speak the language of the other, the more your own eyes find the doors of a mysterious castle opening, and every door will lead to a chamber full of treasures and jewels.

Thus the mystery of tender familiarity begins with the desire to know, learn, and experience more and more about the other. And the more we begin to understand about the other, the more strongly grows the longing to go still further and further into that person's uncharted depths, to experience more and more, to hear and understand ever more deeply the mystery of the other. The initial shyness is transformed into curiosity. The anxious flight, the need to keep one's distance, turns into an increasingly strong need to be close to one another. What in the beginning was a furtive glance from far off now yearns to sink into the eyes of the other as if into the ocean, and with increasing ardor that person's essence pervades one's nights and dreams, continually present. It is as though from this point on the whole world had entered into a symbolic relationship with the other, as if that person's soul were spreading over all the earth, transforming everything into a part of the beloved's body, to express itself in it and place itself there here and now. It's as though the entire world had become a sacrament of the other's love, a sign of the beloved's beatific nearness.

You can no longer see the clouds in the sky without sending them greetings to pass on to the beloved. You can't hear the rivers rush without hearing the beloved's voice. The stars at night shine like her eyes, the band of the Milky Way has the golden shimmer of her hair, and all the flowers of the field stretch out like a carpet beneath her feet.

In this poetry of love the magical fairy tales of the shamans describe an earth where the trees, the stones, the animals speak to them of the distant beloved at the end of the world on the glass mountain, of the goddess of heaven, and the secret center of the world.[16] All their wanderings were only stages for them, all places of rest were only way stations en route to her, and the whole world was shot through with the encantatory magic of her love. The longer this continual search, this "taming" of the other, this ripening familiarity of love lasts, the more richly and complexly do the memory of shared experience and the poetry of tenderness fuse with the form and essence of the other. It's as if the world consisted of an invisible field of force, all of whose lines lead to the heart of the other. And even the things that once seemed so indifferent, as the field of wheat necessarily seems to the fox, now take on the coloring and meaning of this symbolic magic of love. Even the things in us we thought we had to exclude from our lives because we thought them dangerous — "wild" or "animalistic" — become friendly, domesticated, things we can live with. The fox, as a symbol of the unconscious, himself pleads for the gift of "taming."[17]

But love transforms more than spatial things; above all it turns temporal experience into a magic ring, with the rhythm of farewell, expectation, and encounter playing around it like a filigree of strung pearls. In love the time till the next rendezvous often seems to stretch out endlessly. In the moments of happy oneness time seems to stand still, and parting is always linked to the sure promise to come back as soon as possible. What might be considered, outside the bounds of love, drearily boring – the continual repetition, the eternal return of the same – is shaped by love into bliss and duty. Desire keeps driving the lovers together and divides time into the cycle of a feast, with phases of devoted preparation and phases of fulfillment, when the waiting is rewarded. All friendship is subject to the law of such ceremonies – a ritual hallowing of shared time, in order to join in the mutual internal creation of the other's presence.

All purely external acquaintanceships, all cocktail party friendships, all marriages in which love has died, all social contacts dedicated strictly to one's status and career instead of the person of the other, are afflicted by the same trouble: They all end up going under along the well-worn rails of time. Or it's as if time were a clockwork whose wheels, with mechanical precision, grind and shatter all enthusiasm, all surprises, all fantasy and joy. Outside of love all human relationships unravel and turn into mere accumulations of "dates," "meetings," "occasions."

Only love has the power to prevent daily encounters from becoming everyday matters. Only love preserves intimate familiarity from habitual contempt. Only love saves regularity from routine, continual repetition from inner erosion, solid agreements from imperceptible sclerosis. Love alone rejuvenates and constantly recreates. It liberates what is still undeveloped; it shapes what is still waiting to be formed. It sets free from imprisonment what may lie trapped under the burden of guilt and fear. It gives the gift of an infinite curiosity and joy in the being of the other.

Thus love is the only effective antidote to boredom; it's the sanctification of time in ritual and ceremony. In Saint-Exupéry's view, this notion of a temporal and spiritual architecture of life within the "human desert" — in the face of the empty sifting of time into the void of an hourglass — plays an enormous role. As the "Berber lord" explains in *Citadel:* "Just as the cathedral is a certain configuration of stones, which are all alike, but are distributed according to lines of force, whose structure speaks to the spirit, in just the same way there is also a ceremony of my stones. And the cathedral is more or less beautiful. Likewise the liturgy of my year is a certain configuration of days that at first are all alike, but are distributed according to lines of force. . . . And even so there is a ceremony for features of the face. . . . There is a ceremony of my village, because look, today is a feast day, or the death knell is ringing, or it is the hour for the grape harvest, or it's time to get together and build the wall, or the community is suffering from famine. . . . And I don't know anything in the world that wasn't at first a ceremony. Don't expect anything from a cathedral without architecture, a year without feast days, a face without symmetry. . . . You wouldn't even know what to do with your pile of materials."[18]

"Thus I came a step closer to knowing happiness and agreed to pose it to myself as a problem. For it appeared to be the fruit of choosing a ceremony creating a happy soul, rather than a sterile gift of vain objects."[19]

The quite similar remark that the fox makes to the Little Prince about love's ceremonies, its regular duties and the structure of its order, has nothing intrinsically new about it. But now he realizes what he was doing every morning when he cleaned the volcanoes on his planet and cleared away the roots of the baobab tree, a constantly repeated chore that preserved the molten interior of the planet, the world of instinctual desires, from becoming "explosive," and at the same time refused to put up with any "growths" whose excess would necessarily destroy life. This is a symbolic description of the consistent hygiene of the ego in touch with its own emotions as well as with its own claims on itself. These are the first preliminary exercises in self-discipline on the way to love. They show us something else that the Little Prince unconsciously learned in his painstaking dealings with the rose: that people and things become valuable on account of the time we spend on them.

This is true of all encounters with anyone or anything, and it's the experience that Saint-Exupéry ardently sought to gain as the lesson of the desert: to be able to understand that the preciousness of water comes from the starlit march to the well. It's not consumption but commitment and effort, sacrifice, and the persistence of the desert itself, as Saint-Exupéry sees it, that make us human. The world can recover its unity only if it accepts this challenge. Saint-Exupéry has the ruler in *Citadel* say: "Then the miracle will happen, although someone whom I assign to your caravan – if he doesn't understand your language and doesn't share in your fears, your hopes, or your joys . . . – will meet only an empty desert. So he'll spend the whole time yawning, as he crosses an endless surface that simply bores him. And nothing in my desert will change this traveler. The well will strike him as just another medium-sized hole in the ground, from which you have to shovel the sand away. And what would he have learned from boredom, since it's by nature invisible? Because it's nothing but a handful of grains blown by the wind, although that's enough to transform everything for the man bound to it, the way salt transforms a banquet. And my desert, if I just show you the rules of the game, will gain such power over you and enthrall you so, that I can choose you, however banal, egotistical, suspicious, and skeptical you may be, in the suburbs of my city or the stagnation of my oases, and impose on you one journey across the desert, to make the man in you burst forth. . . . And if I have done no more than get you to share in the language of the desert — because what is essential is not things, but from the meaning of things — the desert, like a sun, will have made you sprout and grow."[20]

In exactly the same way we learn from the Little Prince's environment that "water may also be good for the heart."[21] On the verge of dying of thirst, as Saint-Exupéry describes himself in an autobiographical passage from *Wind, Sand, and Stars,* at the outermost extreme of existence, even the question of physical survival loses its meaning.[22] The only issue is to explain how we live and die.

In this we can see a peculiar, characteristically Saint-Exupéryan linkage of love and death. Both demand total engagement from the individual. Both call for a total decision about existence. Both show existence in its unveiled reality. And just as love transforms everything in the world into a sacrament, into the symbolic presence of the beloved, so in the face of death all things become symbols of existential density and profundity. "Still waters" (Ps. 23:2) appear in the Bible as an image of a life that has cast off the concerns of ensuring mere subsistence and has learned to live from deeper "sources." In the same way

the "waters of life" are a frequent symbol in both the language of religion and of fairy tales, designed to show how
people find their way from a superficial attitude toward
life to a new inner beginning.[23] Rebirth and purification,
protection-support and originality, depth and fertility are
all bound together in the image of the well. In the final analysis, however, the image of the well means the definitive
stripping away of all husks, consenting to death, returning
to the stars — and the Little Prince knows this.

Chapter 4

Of Love and Death, or the Window on the Stars

CB

T HE CONVERSATION WITH THE FOX has ultimately left the Little Prince with a crucial new
realization: "I am responsible for my rose."[1] Everything that Saint-Exupéry has to say about love, life, and
death, using the whole palette of symbolic religious language, culminates in this one point: The meaning of things
does not lie in themselves but in their interconnection,
which is disclosed through the exchange of mutual relationship and responsibility. But for the Little Prince this
means having to take his departure from the world and
returning to his rose, which he had so guiltily left behind. And this return means his death. His time is up. The
measure of his stay on earth is full.

What happens when a person whom we love dies? We
will never really grasp this event. It can abruptly and irre-
vocably sever the closest bonds of friendships: Before our
very eyes a person collapses whom we wanted to hold on
to and carry with us for a lifetime. In the middle of a con-

61

versation the words die away on our friend's lips. A cold stiffness replaces the most charming beauty and the most soulful expression. While medicine can explain it, death baffles human understanding. At best we can formulate some conditions under which death seems acceptable as a part of life. And these are evidently the same prerequisites for life's making sense in human terms.[2] Rightly viewed, death is like a keystone, a summary of all the rules that govern the unfolding of love in our lives.

One might be inclined to accept the Buddhist doctrine of abjuring love in order to anticipate and escape the grief of all transitory existence. If you love nothing, you'll never be caught by pain in the face of death.[3] This theory sounds wise, but it robs life of its meaning, its structure and coherence. The sadness of earthly departures is a part of love, yet it alone can give an answer to the enigma of dying.

First of all, love provides an answer to death, if only by experiencing the strange ritual of time to which everything is subject, and which demands its own special sort of obedience. After precisely one full year the Little Prince prepares himself for death. The cycle of time is inexorable. It requires that all events cease in their turn when the moment is ripe. The hour of death is as fixed as the time of sunset. Thus the idea is not to flee death, but to recognize the point in time when death is waiting and obediently to meet it halfway, despite all our anxiety. Only in this manner does death lose its creaturely terror. The snake whose venom kills is also in a way a natural symbol of renewal and a fresh start – a circle that closes, linking the beginning and the end. Only by thinking about this temporal cycle does the fleeting nature of every individual fit into the meaning and patterned flow of the whole.[4] The cycle of nature does not know death; it merely changes the agents and bearers of life that are found at the individual nodal points of the cycle of time.

The meaning of human life is shaped within this sort of temporal ritual, somewhat perhaps as the Mayan Indians imagined each individual day as a deity who shoulders a certain burden in the morning, carries it all through the day, and lays it down at night, before another deity takes it up again the next morning.[5] Thus the death of the individual person becomes a sort of spoke in a wheel, one of the many points that maintain and make possible the course of the cosmos.

In the ritual of time, therefore, death takes on a first glimmer of meaning. "It is only when we become conscious of our part in life, however modest," says Saint-Exupéry in *Wind, Sand, and Stars,* "that we shall be happy. Only then will we be able to live in peace and die in peace, for only this lends meaning to life and to death. Death is sweet when it comes in its place, when it is part of the order of things, when the old peasant of Provence, at the end of his reign, remits into the hands of his sons his parcel of goats and olive-trees, that they in their turn may transmit them to their sons. . . . Each life in turn bursts like a pod and sends forth its seed. . . . One does not die on a farm: their mother is dead, long live their mother!"[6]

From this standpoint death loses the terror of a meaningless imposition when it is experienced from within as serving a larger concomitant whole. So the Little Prince doesn't actually die; he merely returns to his rose, yielding to the moment of death since the time has come to go home.

Still we are left with sadness over what has been lost: To all the living, death appears as a destroyer of joy, a thief who steals the laughter from our lips, the angel with the flaming sword where Paradise ends and banishment begins. Even if the dying person voluntarily submits to the inevitable, for everyone who accompanies that person all the way to the "wall," hoping to protect him or her from the poison of the "snake," death means an utter disappointment, a cynical offense to our feelings,[7] a crude and senseless act of violence. Love instinctively rebels against death. It refuses to accept it, seeking to embrace the other and to hide him or her from death, as if it wanted to use its own body and soul to cover the beloved with a magic cloak, to conceal the beloved from the eyes of the "snake." Measured against the facts of our earthly destiny, this attempt must always end in failure.

And yet love does know a way to be reconciled with death. Only love knows at every moment that the body is only the outer sheath, the husk, and the vessel of a greater life. Love constantly observes the body's gestures as a possible expression of the soul. Love seeks to intuit the inner surface of psychic meaning in all things, in "facts." And instead of protesting against death, love can also look upon it as a symbol of definitive spiritualization. As Saint-Exupéry sees it, death makes it possible to release love, as it were, from the place where it first appeared, and from then on to experience it as a cosmic background in all things: One perceives love as a mysterious music of the spheres, as an inaudible melody that will continue to resound in the language of longing. The Little Prince's star can't be recognized with terrestrial eyes; it's only a dust particle in the universe. But precisely for this reason its light will be scattered over everything that gleams and responds in the nights of sadness. And *because* we, his partners in love, can no longer see or hear him, his laughter will echo along the delicate heartstrings that span the gamut from grief to

yearning. For Saint-Exupéry the color of the wheat field
has changed ever since it came to remind us of the Little
Prince's golden hair. The taste of water has changed ever
since we traveled with him in the desert on the way to the
wellspring. And lonely nights at the window shine more
brightly once we have shared them with the memory of a
distant happiness.

This is the deepest point to which we can take the in-
ternalization of Saint-Exupéry's message on the mystery of
love and death. And yet this concluding thought in *The
Little Prince* contains the most radical and at the same
time probably the most dubious summit of his feeling for
life, his vision of the world, and his poetry of love and
death.

To be sure, the world will look different, depending
upon whether we know the person we love best to be
happy or not. It can be a paradise when it brings word
of our beloved's joy, and it seems a hell when it reports
our beloved's suffering, perhaps without our being able
to do anything about it. The whole happiness of love is
knowing that the person we love above all else is happy.
We will take a thousand roads to find this "wellspring" of
our beloved's happiness, and ultimately the joint search,
the shared journey, will bind us to one another with infinitely greater depth than the moment of pleasure itself.
Or, conversely, that moment of fulfillment will have gained
infinite value precisely because of the effort it took to walk
together through the "wilderness." And yet, and yet: Why
did Saint-Exupéry so vehemently fight shy of recognizing
that love doesn't simply want fidelity, but union, not just
journeying together but dwelling together, not just longing for the unattainable, but eternal fulfillment? Since he
praised the infinite value of friendship the way no other

poet or writer in this century has done, why did he have to deny the infinity of life in friendship?

Normally it's unfair to apply standards of religious truth to a work of literature. But Saint-Exupéry thought of all his work as prophetic. He understood his message as a last bastion for threatened humanity. And so we have to ask how much weight his convictions will bear. Furthermore the fairy tale of *The Little Prince* makes use of so many religious figures that we absolutely must examine the degree to which the content of the symbolic religious language in this story is "cashed in" or discounted. Finally, the tale of the Little Prince leads to the very same question that religion too feels a basic obligation to answer: the question of the meaning of dying and the possibility of love in the face of death. Here, where literally everything is at stake, Saint-Exupéry himself undoubtedly intended to test the claims of his message in the light of the conditions and experiences of his own existence.

Not the least reason for the popularity of *The Little Prince* is the fact that the images used at the conclusion of the story seem to pick up the familiar religious belief in the immortality of the human person. But appearances are deceiving. Saint-Exupéry's starry heavens have only a metaphorical link with the heaven of believers. The Little Prince's departure doesn't promise immortality, just the chance not to lose sight of the dream of a pristine (original) humanity, a chance, despite all failure, despite all finitude, not to betray the values of friendship amid the human desert. "For love is strong as death. . . . Its flashes are flashes of fire, a most vehement flame" (Song. of Sol. 8:6). Saint-Exupéry's truth will go as far as this line in the Old Testament. But what are we to make of love's sadness in the face of death?

This question has once again to be put to Saint-Exupéry, because it can't suffice to transform the person of the beloved into a mere symbol for the value of personal love. And it's not enough to find consolation in melancholy poetry for the death of someone we love more than anything in the world. Admittedly, a great deal is gained when the windows open up and the nights awake from their dreamlessness. A great deal is achieved when once again people come forth whose longing and memory make others laugh. And a great deal is accomplished when we succeed in hearing once again the inaudible sound of the stars in the night (see Ps. 19). But what sort of answer is life left with so long as the Little Prince, a dream figure and nothing more, returns to a distant planet out of loyalty to a flower that, unlike the Romantics, we will seek in vain on earth? Granted, *The Little Prince* teaches us, after a fashion, to rediscover the preciousness of things, to accept the majesty of death and the rhythm of transitoriness as a part of life. But longing isn't hope, waiting isn't expectation, a dream isn't lived reality, the path isn't the goal; and so everything depends on having faith in the yearning of friendship and the certainty of love that the most powerful subjective passion is objective truth.

If it's possible and uniquely worthy of human life to love at least one person infinitely, then love has no greater hope nor truer demand than that human life be immortal. Love insists then that the person whose nature and value we find incomparable and unique, the one in whom all the happiness in the world is concentrated and focused, should live forever, and that our beloved's death should be only a temporary departure.[8] If it is great enough, love has the power of a metaphysical proof, and its language always sounds like that of Edgar Allen Poe's "Annabel Lee," where the poet sings of the death of his supremely beloved niece and bride, Virginia. For weeks Poe spent every day and night at her deathbed, and when she died he fell prey once and for all to physical and psychic ruin.[9] Let me cite the last two stanzas of "Annabel Lee," because it expresses better than any other poem I know the sadness and hope of love in the face of death:

> But our love it was stronger by far than the love
> Of those who were older than we —
> Of many far wiser than we —
> And neither the angels in Heaven above
> Nor the demons down under the sea,
> Can ever dissever my soul from the soul
> Of the beautiful Annabel Lee.
>
> For the moon never beams without bringing me dreams
> Of the beautiful Annabel Lee;
> And the stars never rise
> But I see the bright eyes
> Of the beautiful Annabel Lee;
> And so, all the night-tide, I lie down by the side
> Of my darling, my darling, my life and my bride,
> In her sepulchre there by the sea —
> In her tomb by the side of the sea.[10]

In fact love's longing is so "unwise," so "young," and so "romantic" that it absolutely must believe in eternal life, lest it lose faith in itself. It never stops caressing the beloved with the tenderest words, and when, illumined by the moon or stars, it feels and remembers the glow of her eyes and the shimmer of her hair, it yearns to believe, and be united with, the other *as living*. After all, in the eyes of the lover the beloved is like a sea that carries one over to the farther shore. And to the lover her death is seen only as a departure and going away to prepare a dwelling on the other side for the one left behind – and there she waits (cf. John 14:1–4).

Thus the Egyptians, the wisest people of all in the ways of eternity, called the act of dying a "landing" on the shore of eternity.[11] And their jackal-headed god Anubis, who accompanies the mourning Isis, not only embodies the "fidelity" of love, but he also knows about the immortality of the beloved. When a person dies, the Egyptians thought, that person's body sinks into the realm of the god Osiris, but the soul rises to the heavens like a bird into the kingdom of the sun, up to the hosts of the stars. The Egyptians painted the image of the soul itself, the *ba*-bird, as a winged creature with a human face; and alongside it they sketched in, by way of explanation, the hieroglyphs for incense, which literally mean, "makes its way to God,"[12] as if the ascent of the soul to heaven was like a prayer, a song of praise, like the fragrance of the grains of incense, which reveal their essence when they burn in the sacrificial fire.

Love's most decisive hope is that we shall see one another again, and this hope shapes the belief in immortality. Just as on earth all things turn into symbols of the beauty and nearness of a person whom we love with all our heart, so conversely love "solidifies" into the certainty that the soul of the other means and contains all things, as love itself has already cut a window onto infinity. A person whom we love from the bottom of our hearts doesn't withdraw into death, as Saint-Exupéry describes the Little Prince doing, into an unreal and inaccessible sphere beyond human experience, like a sort of light that shines forth in all things though it no longer forms a unified *source* of illumination.

Instead, the hope and expectation of love remains that

after a short period of separation we will find our way back
to one another beyond time. There is an inscription on
an Egyptian amulet from the tomb of Tutankhamen ("the
living image of the god Amen") that captures this idea
with unsurpassable beauty. It is the wish of the dead man's
wife, Anches-en-Amen ("she lives for Amen"): "I have loved
you, great Tutankhamen, and my grief that you have gone
is great. But forget that time is time, because after time
we shall see one another once more." Without this absolute hope in eternity and immortality, love would actually
die before its time. Hence Joseph von Eichendorff (1788–
1857) was right to find death less terrible than that lovers
should be arbitrarily torn from each other on earth. He
writes:

> We should call parting death,
> For who knows whither we go, —
> Death is but a short separation,
> And we soon will be meeting again.[13]

Even death can't separate the lovers. On the contrary the
destruction of love would be worse than death. So everything depends upon taking love and friendship themselves
with their hopes and wishes as a proof of truth: The love
of the beloved is immortal, and we will meet again.

But the end of *The Little Prince* is far removed from
this sort of attitude. It has only a superficial resemblance
to the feeling that, Novalis, for example, had for his beloved
Sophie, who died all too young. He thought of her as a visible, palpable incarnation of Cosmic Reason. And it's right
at this point, when the Little Prince returns to his rose,
that we find the fundamental difference between religious
symbolism and poetic metaphor. When he looked up to the
stars at night, Saint-Exupéry wasn't really thinking about

an eternal, indestructible life of love. For him the departure of the Little Prince amounted to the elevation of his figure to a transcendental ideal, of the sort one encounters only fleetingly on this earth and whose return to earth we can warmly desire but scarcely hope for.

By contrast, when Novalis went on his daily trip to his beloved's grave, he considered the love he had experienced on earth as a harbinger of eternity, as the beginning of the kingdom of heaven.[14] He himself was viewed by his contemporaries as a wonderful, pure child, as the incarnation, so to speak, of the Little Prince. Accordingly he thought of the resurrection of the dead as an absolutely certain fact of love. But for Saint-Exupéry the Little Prince embodies only the dream of a life as it actually should have been lived, but had long ago been prematurely destroyed. Thus all religious symbols, especially the symbols of immortality and love's eternal life, are transformed into melancholy reminders of one's own lost hope, or into human postulates that are now powerless to maintain the inner conviction that the reality one demands is real.

One might at first think that Saint-Exupéry's dissolution of symbolic religious language into mere poetic code names was an unavoidable consequence of the progressive exhaustion of religion in our time. In fact, Saint-Exupéry did suffer from the disintegration of the meaning-figures from the past. And his work was basically intended to impart the old symbolic language in a new literary form — a refutation of the dirge for religion in Nietzsche's *Thus Spoke Zarathustra*.[15] If he nevertheless thought it impossible to pick up the old images in their reality, this peculiar ambivalence vis-à-vis the traditional symbols of religion must have been rooted in Saint-Exupéry's experience and personality. And such roots can't be simply a reflection of his day and age but definitely have to be psychologically conditioned.

Actually *The Little Prince* is, not just religiously, but above all psychologically, a nostalgic reference to a lost truth rather than a presentation or even a new realization of this truth. From the psychological standpoint, Saint-Exupéry's symbolic language goes so far as to name the causes of its shattered condition: These are, as we shall immediately see, the same reasons that prevent *The Little Prince* from ending the way a "proper" fairy tale absolutely has to end.

A fairy tale narrative with a psychologically satisfying conclusion simply couldn't leave us, as Saint-Exupéry's does, with the crashed flyer (the narrator's ego) accompanying the Little Prince to the well, only to be instantly separated from the Prince by his death. In fairy tales the story must somehow or other have a mysterious woman dwelling by the "well of life," waiting to be rescued.[16] It has to show how dangerous it is dive into the depths down to the enchanted beloved. Mysterious doors have to swing open, and the hero must endure the menace of dangerous predatory beasts guarding the entrance to a hidden palace. Then there will generally be an adventurous return journey before finally, as a reward for all his toil and trouble, the happy prospect of marriage with the fairy-like magic princess.[17]

Naturally this archetypal succession of themes can be varied, combined, and modulated in endlessly different ways. But in any event, to bring the fairy tale of the Little Prince to a satisfactory finish, the story must show how it's possible to find and experience love and fidelity *here on earth*. Thus for the crashed flyer there could be a real transformation only if the encounter with his own background figure, the Little Prince, were to prepare him for an encounter with an enchanting, bewitching woman whom he can love more than anything else. Thus, for example, Anthony Quinn tells in his autobiography *The Original Sin* about a profound crisis he went through when he began to see his acting career as one enormous lie: He met a young man who stayed with him until Quinn sensed the capacity for love awakening in him.[18]

But in *The Little Prince* Saint-Exupéry characteristically tells an altogether different story. Granted, here too the author is talking about a serious crisis: The high-flying "Icarus" has crashed, and he meets his alter ego in the figure of a youngster. But the flyer – the writer's own ego – never changes his plans and goals after meeting the Little Prince. On the contrary, he keeps working away, repairing his engine. And at the very moment that he gets the job done, the Little Prince dies. True, the lessons that the fox gave the Little Prince are heeded and written down. But their only visible effect in the story is a feeling of sadness and longing, along with a vague hope that the Little Prince might return to earth after all.

This conclusion to Saint-Exupéry's story is so peculiar that one can't help wondering what actually prevents the Little Prince from realizing his message of love and loyalty on earth. According to Saint-Exupéry, it is precisely his loyalty to the rose that calls the Little Prince back to his lonely little planet. But who is this rose that the Little Prince felt so guilty about leaving behind, and whose life has he to fear for if the sheep doesn't have a muzzle? The mystery of this rose must contain the reason for the strange melancholy, the longing for death that hovers over the story of the Little Prince, and especially its ending.

Part Two

cß

QUESTIONS
AND ANALYSES

Chapter 5

The Mystery of the Rose

☙

A T BOTTOM THE FAIRY TALE of the Little Prince has only a single central mystery – all the rest are additions, deductions, or reactions to it. And this mystery flowers above all in the image of the rose. The rose is responsible for both the hopes and sadness of the sunsets. She brings knowledge of love as well as the frustration of mere longing for love. She lingers in the background of all the remarkable heights and depths, breaks and contradictions in Saint-Exupéry's thinking and writing, where she takes on an almost uncanny magical shape. Of course we can discover this mystery only by looking through the eyes of psychoanalysis, but once we do that it becomes unequivocally clear that the rose is the mystery of the mother.

In a sense the story of the Little Prince can be read as an encoded childhood memory, a sort of private dream of regeneration. Saint-Exupéry wrote this fairy tale, which won him worldwide fame, at a time of personal emptiness and disappointment. It was a moment when his quest for the stars, his bird's-eye view of life, his perspective on the world, had come up against a barrier: The "flyer" had crashed. At such times of crisis your thoughts turn back to the past, linking you to the places where the strands got entangled. You try to clarify your own self-image, which by that time may have become distorted beyond recognition.

And so the failed flyer meets the child, who was never allowed to live in him. With the child symbolic pictures and memories emerge that show how the Little Prince lived before he met grown-ups and had to become a grown-up himself. Every one of these points deserves the closest attention, because this is the only way to understand the many details of *The Little Prince* that shed light on Saint-Exupéry's early childhood and that otherwise would remain wholly unintelligible.

Saint-Exupéry himself admits early on that there was a child inside him who wanted to paint his fantasies and visions, but that people got him to replace this drawing of the inner world with "geography," representation of the outer world.[1] A murdered Leonardo in other words. This fate is already a grim one. But *what* did this child want to draw? That question is more important than the ban on painting, because it leads to layers far below the commonplace opposition between reason and emotion, consciousness and the unconscious, bourgeois conformity and artistic freedom.

Oddly enough, most readers of *The Little Prince* find the image of the elephant inside the snake simply entertaining, and the author certainly intended to make that impression. But if we read this picture *symbolically,* it reveals more about Saint-Exupéry's childhood than we get in all the biographies, which are in too great a hurry to get to Saint-Exupéry the great writer, cultural critic, comrade, and pilot, as if he had never been a child. In fact Saint-Exupéry's work seems practically designed to seduce us into seeing only the grand and completed parts and hastening to forget the Little Prince, that enigmatic figure of repressed possibilities and stifled life.The appearance of this nostalgically transfigured symbol of a pure, innocent childhood makes sense and becomes necessary only to correct and break down the one-sided and now untenable grown-up standpoint of the crashed pilot. If ever it was crucial to inquire about Saint-Exupéry as child and not as an adult, then it's here in the introductory images of *The Little Prince.*

Psychoanalysis is greatly interested in so-called screen memories,[2] the symbolically encoded communications that often condense several years of early childhood into a single scene. This is exactly what Saint-Exupéry appears to have done. He writes of enormous snakes in the sultry tropical jungles swallowing their prey alive. One isolated symbol can never provide infallible insight into any psychic condition. But if we met this image on page one of *The Little Prince* in a child's dream, we would be almost compelled to think that this huge figure of a snake could only be the mother.[3] Then her prey, which she pulls into her jaws, would naturally be her child, the oversized "baby elephant," which was never allowed to be a child. Instead scarcely had it arrived in the world than he had to be "big and strong," in order to satisfy, with his own existence, his mother's hunger for the "substance" of love and life.

Unfortunately, however, grown-ups never see it that way. As often as Saint-Exupéry drew his gigantic boa constrictor that had swallowed the elephant, grown-ups never managed to recognize it except as a hat — protection for the head. And at first glance Saint-Exupéry's childhood must have looked like a thoroughly protected world, surrounded and encased on all sides. Yet from the hidden inner perspective of the child it was a lifelong prison, a never-ending embryonic state, a revised birth.The first time he draws the giant boa, the child loses his confidence in the world of the grown-ups. He fails to make them understand him: They smile and laugh over a childhood tragedy, because they're incapable of "seeing with the heart." They have no idea that what looks "well-protected" to them is basically frightful. And even when shown an "X-ray" of the (mother) snake's digestive tract, they explain all these visions from the jungle as childish phantasms and feverish chimeras. This sort of thing, they say, has to be countered by dealing with the "real" world by way of mental hygiene.

In this way a child's anxieties are soon covered over by purely rational modes of adaptation, and we see the beginning of the double standards and contradictions between an aggressive will to achieve and a strongly repressive longing that run all through Saint-Exupéry's later work.

What can a child do who's suffering but isn't allowed to show it? The child would like to communicate his feelings, but in the name of higher reason he is persistently misunderstood. He feels penned in by invisible walls, but he's continually told that he has imagined the whole thing, that he should busy himself instead with something "sensible." Evidently the young Saint-Exupéry wasn't so discouraged that he completely abandoned his original feeling that he was right. But the destructive work was thorough enough to cause a lot of repression and deformation.

Thus Saint-Exupéry does not, in fact, seem to realize what he was actually saying with his "elephant snake." On the contrary, he playfully aestheticizes the actual dilemma posed by the picture. His real feelings are replaced by quasi-artistic expression. A highly complicated problem in mother-child relations is generalized and abstracted into a question of how *all* children relate to adults. In the process, without a word of commentary, the notion is presupposed (and consequently accepted) that instead of being allowed to express his feelings immediately, a child can at most convey them in a symbolic code. Even when he looks back on his childhood, Saint-Exupéry takes this indirect, "artistic" form of communication so much for granted that he can spike his tale of a painter's "tremendous career" with a goodly dose of self-irony. He does this solely to conceal the deep resignation he must have settled into even as a child: It's impossible to articulate one's thoughts and feelings to grown-ups unless you do it "rationally." Indeed, it amounts to a revenge on the "big people" when you struggle successfully to find a mode of expression that is artistically legitimate and whose symbols are sufficiently encoded to be generally comprehensible and interesting.

It's clear what Saint-Exupéry was sparing himself by living this way: He no longer had to return to the real themes and wounds of his childhood. Above all he avoided the decisive conflict with the "snake." He wasn't forced, as characters in some fairy tales are, to face a fight with the "dragon."[4] But he paid for these "advantages" with strong guilt feelings and inhibitions, with a great deal of repression and resignation, with fear and loneliness, and finally with the tendency to despise himself for his own weakness and others for their imaginary greatness. Self-irony, contempt, and escaping into dreams – all this perpetuates psychic problems instead of solving them. Yet under certain circumstances this very pressure from pain, sensibility, and fantasy gives rise to the sort of persons to whom we are indebted for the most valuable cultural creations on this planet: the artists and priests, the dreamers and ghost-seers, the poets and shamans, the men and women whose memory of the Little Prince can never die. His figure is the secret source of literary achievement. But it's also, for Saint-Exupéry, the symbol of a highly ambivalent bond with the mother.

We need only run through the Little Prince's recollections of the planet of the rose to find plenty of further encoded information about Saint-Exupéry's relationship with his mother — as if to complete the symbol of the giant boa. Of course, we can't simply identify the Little Prince with Saint-Exupéry's childhood. But it's hard to deny that in everything the Little Prince says about his planet we see the condensation of essential impressions from Saint-Exupéry's childhood, and especially the memories of his mother. This was a time long before the Little Prince got to know the whole gamut of the adult world and got a solid footing on the earth, in the world of external reality. And this entire time is stamped with the quiet melancholy of the sunsets, with the ordered loneliness of the cleaned-out volcanoes, and with the relatively late but all the more careful attention to the rose. However fragmentary the Little Prince's description of it may be, the rose is a positive whirlwind of lovableness, affectation, and insistent egotism.

The Little Prince's first remarks mention the helpless and unprotected state of the rose. Even these small bits of information result from his trying not to say anything derogatory about the rose. It seems to me that we would be greatly minimalizing these "childish" reflections if we took them to mean no more than the bromide that every rose has its thorns. If the real topic here were "sheep," "roses," and "thorns" as objects or metaphors of nature, then we'd basically have no idea of what to make of the passage than to call it one more example of the droll fantasy of an innocent child. But in fact it undoubtedly describes the conflict and ambivalence of a central human relationship. The superficial harmlessness of this description immediately disappears once we recall that here we have a child speaking, however cryptically, about the person whom he loves more than anything. This person can only be his mother; all other hypotheses would take us outside the situation where the Little Prince really lives: in the time of his childhood.

But with respect to his own mother the Little Prince's question is a highly alarming signal. We realize at once why the problem was so important to him: *Why does the rose have thorns?* Why, in other words, can his mother, who is on the whole so lovable and loving, be so piercing, so cutting, so full of barbs? Though otherwise so admirable that you simply want to stroke and caress her, she can still, when you least expect it, hurt you in a surprisingly deceitful fashion. Why?

Of course, this is a question that the child must ask himself and come up with an answer for. His mother's behavior is so obviously contradictory, confusing, and ambiguous that it can't be readily explained. As he thinks things over, the Little Prince has one sacrosanct assumption: that his mother really is, in and of herself, a "rose," the quintessence of beauty, charm, and sweetness. There can be no doubts about this, her true nature. But if his mother can nevertheless be so completely different, this must have special reasons, and it's the child's job to discover them.

The most obvious answer to the Little Prince's central problem would unquestionably be the one offered by the flyer: Roses grow their thorns out of spite.[5] If this were true, the mother would be responsible for her wounding attacks. And the child in turn would have something like a duty to defend himself and to be heartily "bad" to mother. But the Little Prince is utterly outraged at that very possibility, and it sounds as if he's simply echoing the scorn with which his mother previously greeted his own invective: "You're mixing everything up together, you're confusing everything!"[6]

In fact the whole mother-son symbiosis would be in extreme danger, if the Little Prince ever dared to voice certain doubts about his mother's kindness and blamelessness. Thus he has to look for explanations that cleanse his mother's image of all suspicion. Otherwise he himself would momentarily become one of the bad "big people," who are so horribly insensitive, so superficial and vain. He would cease to be his mother's "dear little" Prince, the golden royal child, as Saint-Exupéry himself has painted him: with the rakishly lowered giant thorn of his dagger and the huge blue cloak with the red lining, in which his mother protects him, as if she were a heavenly queen from another planet holding him in her lap. This is the positive counter-image of the giant boa,[7] an image designed to seem as sweet as possible, but clinging to it carries a heavy penalty: The Little Prince must constantly defend his mother from his own observations, and his general amnesty for maternal "thorns" will forever dictate that his mother is after all "only" weak — guileless, defenseless, helpless. And the Little Prince himself will therefore have to keep an eye on his mother. He himself will have to look after her solicitously and do everything imaginable for her. Shielded in the cloak of his queen, he will enter the lists for his mother's honor and protection. This is a highly exhausting double role, in which, by playing the protected protector, the child must basically take the place of her husband in order to be loved by his mother.

In fact we may well suspect that the Little Prince's stories about the planet of the rose, down to the least details, are Saint-Exupéry's coded autobiographical memories. In rereading *The Little Prince* it's always a surprise to note that the rose doesn't appear on the planet until relatively late. Till then the Little Prince was evidently living in an unbroken mutual union with his mother, and the globular pictures that Saint-Exupéry paints of the planet seem in this context to condense specific infant fantasies of security and love.[8] This is a time when his mother did not yet exist as a real "opposite number." But even at this early point certain anal demands for cleanliness and order – the "volcano sweeping" – have to be strictly observed.[9]

Only at a later stage does the mother come on the scene in the figure of the helpless-thorny rose. There is a good deal of evidence that behind this event, which will shape the Little Prince's life for years, lies the death of Saint-Exupéry's father, which occurred when the boy was just four years old.[10] This marks a phase of psychic development in which the bonds, conflicts, and ambivalence between a boy and his mother take on a peculiar intensity anyhow. Once the Oedipus complex is resolved, they will essentially determine the shape of his conscience in later years. In any event from this perspective we can understand the whole climate on the planet of the rose: the melancholy and loneliness, the exclusivity and tender admiration with which the Little Prince dedicates himself to the rose, the exaggerated sense of duty to be responsible for and protect her. The question is now simply: What is it that the rose actually has to protect herself or be protected from?

It would be easy enough to imagine all sorts of dangers that might threaten the rose on the Little Prince's planet, but none of them actually applies. The menace of the baobab tree — that the Little Prince might become too proud, too forward, or arrogant — has long been eliminated through his daily chores. Nor could one seriously worry that a "tiger," say, might live on the Little Prince's planet — should the Little Prince be too aggressive and rough.[11] The only real threat materializes when, after a longish separation, the Little Prince returns to the planet of the rose with his sheep.

The symbol of the sheep is likewise rather ambiguous, and it can't be read rightly until one applies it to Saint-Exupéry's relationship with his mother. Otherwise it's bound to look downright absurd. The Little Prince knows, of course, that a sheep is stupid enough to eat a rose. Why in heaven's name, then, does he always take a sheep along with him to his planet? How is it that the flyer has to draw him a picture of such a sheep? Why can't he paint for himself whatever he wants? And can a *drawing* of a sheep eat roses?

These sorts of questions have to be discarded as typical grown-up obtuseness. The answer is that for a child even a sketch of a sheep is a real sheep. But this doesn't explain the whole scene; it simply denies that it's unusual. The truth, evidently, is that the Little Prince must himself slip into the role of the "lamb" in order to live by his mother's side. Should any conflict arise he will have to pronounce himself, and not his mother, the guilty party. To be innocent himself he has to transform himself into a sheep. Whenever he fails to understand his mother's thorny mannerisms, that has to be understand as a consequence of his "stupidity." Whenever his mother hurts him, that must be thought of simply as a result of his forward, fresh behavior. The sheep absolutely requires a muzzle, lest it eat the rose, the way the giant snake ate the elephant.[12]

This rethinking creates stress for the child that ultimately prevents him from simply being a child. It lays a responsibility on him that would make most adults come to grief. But Saint-Exupéry apparently pulled off this stunt in his childhood, at least up to a certain point: He fashioned an extraordinarily adult way of thinking so that he could remain his mother's child. He asked the flyer to draw a sheep for the Little Prince, a sheep that had no horns[13] and that would instantly present his mother with a double joy: Despite everything he won't seem too "old" or too "precocious," too melancholy, sad, or sick, *and* he will owe his fantastic existence to the sole fact that he remains safely guarded in the "chest," protected in his mother's womb.

The nightmare of the elephant inside the giant snake has turned, in the very next scene, into an express wish, a positive need. From now on his only concern will be how to tie up the sheep's mouth — one careless moment, and the rose's life could be threatened.[14] None of the Little Prince's worries is greater than this one. All his attention is focused on it, and his own death in the end is not so bad as the unceasing frightful possibility of killing the defenseless rose with a false word. If she died, the whole world would be finished, and all the stars extinguished too.[15] Saint-Exupéry has, thank God, something to ward off this danger, a power that can comfort the Little Prince and cradle him in safety: The rose isn't in serious danger — so long as he keeps an eye on the sheep and muzzles it. One single thoughtless, stupid word could be fatal to his mother.

Proof that this Oedipal reconstruction of the Little Prince's world is on the right track can be gotten — in detail – from the further accounts of the rose itself. When she appears at sunrise, like the Egyptian god Nefertem, who arises out of the lotus,[16] she always first attends to her morning toilette with voluptuous insistence and seductive slowness. Obviously the Little Prince is discovering for the first time his mother's womanly beauty. And however alien the rose's vanity may seem to him, however strange her demands, she nevertheless stirs in him a fascination that has to be labeled sensual, along with an astonished, spellbound admiration. This impression also says a good deal for the assumption that the blooming of the rose is closely bound up with experiences Saint-Exupéry had in his early sexual development.

Still, the peculiar dilemma of the mother-child relationship in Saint-Exupéry's life probably doesn't lie mainly in the realm of sex. His work does have enough descriptions of woman as *femme fatale,* at once alluring and frightening. And these images *are* only marginally compensated for by the stereotypical image of woman as mother.[17] Furthermore the reader will search in vain through Saint-Exupéry's *oeuvre* for passages where a man and a woman make even a stab at real dialogue. But in *The Little Prince* at least the crucial point is not actually the Oedipal theme, but rather the mother's thoroughly depressive darkening of all vital impulses with the strangest and most incomprehensible expectations. Linked to that, on the Little Prince's part, is a constant flow of guilt feelings and self-reproach.

For example, scarcely has the rose awakened in the morning than she likes to have breakfast, and the Little Prince has to wait on her with a sprinkling can full of fresh water. The tone in which the rose gives orders sounds extremely solemn, aristocratic, and affected. Any gesture of insubordination would amount to an act of *lèse-majesté*. This behavior by the rose is all the more conspicuous because at every possible opportunity Saint-Exupéry has the Little Prince positively reveling in contempt for the hollow vanity and senseless self-importance of grown-ups. Only in the case of the rose are all the opening lines of potential criticism that must have been on the tip of his tongue abruptly cut short.

There is no shaking the impression that the vehement contempt with which the Little Prince more or less drenches the grown-ups around him may originally have been meant for his rose. But here he fell prey to the censorship of the "muzzle." So we have a displacement of the criticism, designed to protect the image of his mother from any injury. This, however, only deepens the guilt feelings and ambivalence that already exist between mother and child.

Above all the rose proves to have a downright unnatural sensitivity to "drafts" and "atmospheric shifts." It sounds both tragic and grotesque when the Little Prince has to provide the rose with a glass cover and a folding screen so she doesn't catch cold. To prevent his mother from coming down with a cold or getting a stuffy nose, the child must constantly keep her surrounded by a protective area. And he has to do this without even understanding why. The rose does attempt to explain to the Little Prince that her sensitivity is due to her "special origin." But the Little Prince is quite right to think this is a pure pretext that explains nothing and is designed simply to put him in the wrong. Yet even here he can't raise any objections. He has to submit completely to the rose's moods. All she has to do is to cough, and he will be assaulted by guilt and remorse.[18] The image of the giant boa and the elephant, which at the outset could be given only a vague interpretation, now reveals its contents.

Given the conditions he has to work under – his mother is always right, even when she's wrong; if he wants to contradict his mother, he's a "sheep"; and every kind of backtalk is a mortal insult – the difficulties the Little Prince has with his mother are a priori unsolvable. On the contrary, you can twist and turn on the planet of the rose as much as you want, but you'll never escape the feeling that all the goodwill in the world won't enable you to do what's right. Meanwhile she, the poor, powerless, helpless rose has, in fact, not just thorns but real tiger's claws.[19]

As if in passing, the Little Prince mentions the worst of all maternal weapons: the blackmailing threat to let herself die, so as to fill him with lethal feelings of shame.[20] For a child there is absolutely no more frightening reproach than having to hear that his misbehavior might cause his mother's death. A child would rather consider his own right to life forfeit than do anything that could prompt this charge. But in order not to be threatened with death the Little Prince's rose doesn't just ask for specific behavior that he can clearly understand and carry out. She makes the extravagant, totalitarian demand that he love her boundlessly. What she's chiefly aiming to suppress is any possibility of there being anything near her on her own level or, worse yet, higher. And whenever the suspicion arises that the Little Prince might direct his attention to anything else except his rose, she is always capable of overwhelming him with the guilt feelings of a potential murderer. It doesn't help the Little Prince to have a strong hunch that his rose's depressive coughing fits, her accusations that he's not taking good enough care of her, that he's too cold and loveless, unfaithful and ungrateful, are in the final analysis just a device to guarantee her continued power and influence.[21] The non-stop guilt feelings still remain, fundamentally poisoning the mother-son relationship with their terrible intensity.

As the Little Prince tells himself later on, there could only be one way to live with such a rose-mother: if he could stop taking her words so seriously. Often enough he'd simply have to tune her out or ignore her whims. Alternately he would have to focus all the more intensely on how lovable the rose is in herself, and what a magical atmosphere she can spread about her. He'd have to be able to grasp that her accusations and depression are also expressions (and especially strong ones) of tenderness and love.[22] But to be able to feel that way, one would have to encounter the rose on a free and independent footing. No child, as long as he's a child, could manage that. And so the Little Prince grasps the tragedy of his relation to the rose quite rightly with the staggering words: "I was too young to know how to love her."[23]

At no other time in life is a person so dependent on being loved by, and loving, his or her mother as in childhood. But if you have for a mother a rose that, as on Rilke's tombstone (likewise alluding to his mother), can be understood only as a "pure contradiction,"[24] then in the long run this need for love can never be met. Under certain circumstances you may ultimately have to flee your own mother as a threat to your life. The Little Prince does just that, but again only to find that even while he is escaping, in fact precisely because of this, his guilt feelings are all the more painful. There is no escape from this mother's tiger's talons, from her invisible serpent's jaws.

Scarcely has the Little Prince gotten serious with his silent protest and begun to prepare for his departure when the rose (surprisingly!) acts more brave and selfless than ever before. It's true: She loves the Little Prince more than anything. She wishes him nothing but happiness,[25] and with all her neuralgias and complaints she never wanted it to come to this. Now that the Little Prince is trying to break away from her, it would almost be a relief to hear her come out with her usual reproaches and lamentations. That would offer, at least looking back on it, something like an excuse and justification for the Little Prince's cruel decision to leave his mother behind. Instead the "quiet sweetness"[26] that she puts on display, now of all times, has the effect of an incarnate accusation—which is the whole point.

Indeed, the rose, who has hitherto managed to heap all the guilt one-sidedly on the Little Prince, all of a sudden proves capable of admitting a certain share of guilt in the tragedy of their relationship. And she scolds not just the Little Prince but herself as well for being "stupid."[27] But this belated repentance is not only too late, it is cleverly contrived to deprive the Little Prince's attempted flight of any legitimization. If up till now he has always been guilty because of his "stupidity," he has to endure the worst guilt feelings of all for turning his back on his mother—a mother who's so good, so undemanding, so modest, and above all so understanding.

She understands, of course, that all butterflies have to pass through the caterpillar stage.[28] In other words she accepts the Little Prince's alienation as a necessary chrysalis process. And she tolerates and bears all these bitter moments with such moving patience and empathy. And so the Little Prince will feel very bad if he disregards this self-revelation of how truly good and great his rose is, and sticks to his plan to escape. He is swamped by the deepest repentance and sadness, and finally the rose herself has to force him to put an end to the excruciating departure scene. Meanwhile her permission, indeed her wish, for the Little Prince to create and find his happiness independently of her chains him all the more tightly to the rose than all the oft-voiced accusations and remonstrations have thus far managed to do. From now on the question of her weal and woe will never leave him. To legitimize his decision he will in the future have to prove that while abroad he really *is* meeting with success and happiness. Otherwise he'll only be adding new grief to the rose's painful generosity in giving him up. And even the happiness he's supposed to win will be poisoned by the guilty sense that he bought it with his rose's tears, indeed with the sacrifice of her life.

The reader can easily confirm all these statements about the background of what goes on in *The Little Prince*. All one need do is pay consistent attention to the book's remarks about the planet of the rose, which seem at first so disconnected and peculiarly charming. Above all one has to use the requisite care in exploring their symbolic value by means of psychoanalysis. From this standpoint *The Little Prince* looks like a coded account of a not-so-rosy childhood. It might be called a settling of accounts with the half-conscious or mostly unconscious influences of his loving/distressing mother-rose, or an attempt to find at long last a fair and workable solution to a never-ending dilemma.

All this is done, to be sure, in a cryptic, floating fashion, as if we were allowed to imagine the meaning but not pronounce any verdict. Saint-Exupéry keeps stressing that his Little Prince gives no answer when asked a question,[29] and in a superficial sense this is surely true. But the actual subject of *The Little Prince,* the mystery of the mother, covered over by guilt feelings, anxiety, and ambivalent conflicts, obviously is and remains taboo. And for just this reason it takes a certain symbolic density to disguise from the conscious mind what that mind doesn't want to know. Yet these symbols objectively impart a great deal more than the author would frankly admit to himself.

It is precisely as a symbolic figure, as an image, that the Little Prince, by his mere existence, answers all the major psychological questions. The trick is simply to ask the right ones, or to feel our way into the emotional significance of everything the Little Prince says, till no detail appears superfluous, disparate, or contradictory. Then we'll see how Saint-Exupéry's most famous and important work tells us more about this wonderful and deeply wounded child — the future immortal and widely loved author — than all the biographies and monographs ever could.

But, it might still be objected, couldn't all these interpretations and attempts at psychological reconstruction be based on preconceived opinions or inadequate theoretical and methodological assumptions? Is something humanly great and grand being dragged once again into the mire of "Oedipal fantasies"? Maybe everything was completely different. And finally, who can guarantee the correctness of psychological interpretations anyhow?

It must be stressed that everything I have said so far about the tie binding the Little Prince to his rose was worked out almost exclusively from reading the book. I made little use of other biographical or autobiographical information. And it must further be pointed out that numerous passages from Saint-Exupéry's narrative would have to remain incomprehensible or purely grotesque, unless it could be proved, as I have done, that when seen in the light of a single central complex of problems they are intrinsically valid, necessary, and consistent. This criterion of internal coherence and harmony is a very strong argument for proving the correctness of the interpretations chosen. But even readers who view psychoanalysis with skepticism or incomprehension can be shown the likelihood that there really was in Saint-Exupéry a figure like the Little Prince, with his cares, guilt feelings, anxiety, and sense of duty to his mysterious rose – and that this rose was his mother.

Fortunately we have the letters that Saint-Exupéry wrote to his mother over a period of twenty years. Critics may allege that the novel's meridional French diction can put far more tenderness and poetry into the relations of a boy, a youth, or a grown man than German or English can. Even so, it's moving and surprising to see how for a quarter century, unaltered by education, career, marriage, and war the same feelings of concern, sadness, insecurity, responsibility, dependency, and alleged loyalty find constant, never-changing expression in these letters. And it's quite obvious that these same feelings echo in the remarkable relationship between the Little Prince and his rose. Hence in the following section I'll quote a few dated excerpts from Saint-Exupéry's letters to his mother, and the reader will be readily able to visualize how completely Saint-Exupéry was tied to his mother all his life.

When he wrote his first letters, Saint-Exupéry was twenty-one; he sent his last at age forty-four. Between those dates lies half a human life. But throughout that time in his dealings with his mother Saint-Exupéry remained inalterable, unchangeable, absolutely the same: begging and revering, repentant and contrite, looking for protection and at the same time wanting to play the protector, forever binding his mother's destiny to his own, seeking freedom and still longing to go home – a continual ambivalence, which as an overall impression offers the most eloquent commentary conceivable on the Little Prince's "difficulties" and "feelings of responsibility" toward his rose.

"Mama," Saint-Exupéry writes in 1921, "I read your letter again. You seem so sad and weary to me – and then you reproach me for my silence – Mama. But I did write to you! You seem sad to me, and then I get melancholy. . . . I embrace you, just as I love you, my little Mama."[30] "I also dream a lot about you, and I remember many things about you from when I was little. And it stabs me in the heart that I've given you so much trouble. If you only knew, Mama, how delectable I find you, the finest of all the 'mamas' that I know. And you so much deserved to be happy and then, too, not to have a nasty big boy who growls and storms all day long. Isn't that so, Mama?"[31]   [1921]

"I need you just as much as I did back when I was quite small. The sergeants, the military discipline, the courses on tactics, it's all such dry, brittle stuff! I see you before me, as you arrange flowers in the parlor, and I get furious at them: at the sergeants. How could I make you cry, even a few times? Just thinking about it makes me so unhappy. I made you doubt my tenderness. And yet, if you only knew about it, Mama. You are the best thing I have in life. Tonight I'm homesick like a little boy. When I imagine how you're going about there and talking, and that we could be together and that I'm not getting any of your tenderness and that I'm also no help to you. Tonight I really feel like howling. You are the only consolation when I'm sad. When I was a little boy, I came home with my big knapsack on my back, sobbing because I had been punished – you remember Le Mans, don't you? – And everything could be forgotten only with a kiss from you. You were an almighty protection against the overseers and the Father Prefects. I felt secure in your house, I belonged to you alone, how good that was. Well, now it's just the same, you are my refuge, you know everything, you make me forget everything, and whether I want to or not, I feel like a very little boy."[32]   [1922]

"I'm so sad because I know that you're suffering. . . . I know perfectly well that I should give you all my trust and tell you my cares, so that you can comfort me, as you did when I was little and rattled off all my troubles to you. I know, after all, that you love your son, that tall fellow, so very much."[33]   [1923]

"I put everything in your hands; then you'll speak with the higher powers, and so everything will go well. I'm now like a very little boy; I fly to you for refuge."[34]   [1923]

"For a month now I haven't gotten anything from you. And yet I write often, and this pains me. A word from you would have been welcome to me, because you are, my little Mama, the great love of my heart. When I'm far away, I can see better which friendships are a refuge for me, and word from you, a reminder of you, cures my melancholy."[35]   [1926]

"You are the dearest thing in the world to me. . . . You are far far away from me. And I think about your loneliness. . . . As soon as I come home, I can be a son for you, as I dream of being, and I can invite you to dinner, and give you so many little pleasures. When you came to Toulouse, I felt such grief and shame because I couldn't do anything for you, that I got quite distressed and sullen, and couldn't be tender. But you can tell yourself, my little Mama, that you have filled my life with lovely things the way nobody else ever could have done. And that you are the 'most refreshing' of my memories, the one that most stirs my heart. And the slightest thing of yours that belongs to me warms me inside: your shawl, your gloves – they protect my heart."[36]   [1926]

"If you want, I'll get married...."[37]

"In Le Mans you sometimes sang downstairs, when we were already in bed. That soared up to us like the echo of an enormous feast. That's how it seemed to me. The 'kindest,' the pleasantest object that I ever knew was the little heater in the upstairs room in Saint Maurice. Nothing ever soothed me so much about life.... That little heater protected us from all dangers. Sometimes you came up, opened the door, and found us swathed in cosy warmth. You heard the heater busily humming away and then went downstairs again. I've never had a friend like that. I was taught what eternity is not by the Milky Way, not by flying or the sea, but by the second bed in your room. It was a wonderful stroke of luck to be sick.... That bed was a boundless ocean, to which the grippe entitled me. There was also a crackling fireplace there too. Marguerite taught me what eternity is. I'm not quite sure whether I have lived since my childhood."[38]   [1930]

"I cried when I read your sensible little letter, because in the desert I called out for you. I flared up in tremendous anger against the separation from all people, against this silence, and I called for my Mama. It's terrible when you leave someone behind who needs you, as Consuelo does. You have a powerful longing to go home to protect and defend them. And you tear your nails out on this sand that prevents you from doing your duty, and you'd like to move mountains, and I called for you with the selfishness of a nanny goat. I came home a little bit for Consuelo's sake, but it's through you, Mama, that one comes home. You, with all your weakness, did you know that you are so much the guardian angel, strong and wise, that one prays to you, when one is alone in the night."[39]   [1936]

"And still I hope so much that in a few months you can wrap me in your arms in front of your fireplace, my little Mama, my old Mama, my tender Mama. I hope I can tell you everything I think, can discuss everything with you, contradicting you as little as possible . . . listen to you when you speak to me, you who are always right in all the things of life. . . . My little Mama, I love you."[40]   [1944]

Once again we see in this final letter of Saint-Exupéry an indication of the problem with the little sheep and its muzzle, the problem of the rose, who's right in everything simply because she has to be in the right. Over and beyond that, these letters document the thoughts of duty and loyalty that were so important to Saint-Exupéry, and above all they provide evidence of his strong sense of dependency on the atmosphere of well-being, on the "fragrance" spread by the rose on her little planet. Furthermore these letters demonstrate how intensely Saint-Exupéry was bound up with his mother all his life. Her melancholy reproaches burdened him with guilt feelings and never-ending attempts at reparations. Nevertheless, at the same time she managed through her sensitivity to build him an all-powerful wall of defense against the loveless world outside.

Thus my first impressions in analyzing *The Little Prince* have been more than confirmed. Evidently this was the one strictly concealed side of Saint-Exupéry's nature, the side the world was never supposed to know, that we find expressed in *The Little Prince*. The story is in code, but its language is on the whole much clearer than in any other work by or about Saint-Exupéry himself. We see the unresolved and irresolvable relationship with his mother, with all its longings, ambivalence, demands, and guilt feelings. In other words we will understand the central mystery of the Little Prince, the mystery of the rose, only when we focus our interpretation of it on Saint-Exupéry's mother.

Chapter 6

The Mystery of Icarus

☙

S TILL, THE CHILDISH DEPENDENCY on his mother reveals only one side of Saint-Exupéry, his hidden self. The other, universally visible and admired side of the man is the role of the flyer, the pose of the superior individual, the daredevil, the venturesome thinker, writer, cultural critic, and comrade. In reading over the usual hymns of praise to Saint-Exupéry the flyer,[1] it's easy to miss the fact that it is precisely this role which in *The Little Prince* is waiting to be completed, indeed to be redeemed, by another standpoint: The crash-landing of the flyer opens the fairy tale of *The Little Prince.* To understand properly the symbolic structure of this narrative, we must at the same time seek out which elements in the symbol of the flyer are alive and which are apparently no longer viable. This will provide us with a sort of reverse image of the figure of the Little Prince. And only when we grasp the contrasts and tensions between these two symbolic figures will we see that they constitute Saint-Exupéry's theme and essence, his real pattern and truth. Only by experiencing the tension between the Little Prince and the flyer can we understand why the prophetic promise of Saint-Exupéry's message could never make its way across the melancholy horizon of insatiable longing and proved de facto incapable of moving on to any serene conviction.

In psychoanalysis, just as in Marxian social criticism, there has been no backing away from the old tendency to interpret spiritual attitudes as epiphenomena or responses of certain psychological (or social and economic) complexes. This assumes that the "basis" strictly determines the "superstructure," as if intellectual contents were a product of underlying unconscious processes. Now there is surely no denying that certain theories and life postures can be presented as an ideological translation or rationalization, as a justification or disguise, of unmanageable psychic (or social) incompatibilities.

But in general this supposition scarcely holds up, unless we want to follow a strict ideological party line and declare all intellectual convictions inauthentic, derivative, and deceptive. In point of fact it is impossible to draw conclusions about certain psychic or social complexes simply from their intellectual contents. Instead it's the inconsistencies, logical lapses, and contradictions within any conviction that suggest that certain points of view may be conditioned by some complex. It's not the mind itself, but the "mind-forged manacles," the distortions and disguises of the mind's field of vision, that can at times be interpreted as a consequence of psychic inhibitions and limitations.

As far as Saint-Exupéry's work goes, this means that we are perfectly free to understand and evaluate his "message" positively for his intellectual breadth and human profundity. But that doesn't stop us from asking what somehow or other prevented him from sufficiently trusting his own vision and from adopting in any way except poetically or metaphorically the religious legacy that he defended with so much passion.

No reader of *The Little Prince* can help being struck by the fact that for all its talk about love and loyalty the only warm affection it describes is, peculiarly, in the relationship between the flyer and the Little Prince. This is an almost "Greek" form of homosexual boy-love, in which the role of the young god Eros,[2] the principle of infinite longing, is incarnated in the Little Prince. Nowhere is there any mention of love for a woman, except in the symbol of the rose, which conceals as much as it informs.[3] This fact alone forces us to conclude that, from his boyhood days on, Saint-Exupéry's real love was inalterably given to his "rose." He could best respect and love himself in the role of a loyal child, unspoiled by the grown-up world. At the same time he was too embarrassed to admit to himself and others the full extent of the bond with his mother.

But Saint-Exupéry's fairy tale reveals even more than this. The Little Prince, who loves only his rose, enters this world after being expelled by her, as a refugee from her demands. This contradiction seems to be characteristic of Saint-Exupéry, because his thoughts and emotions are shaped not just by the bond with his mother, with her lofty "conservative" values, but equally by fear of her snake-like constriction. Unless we keep this in mind we'll never understand the deliberate rejection of closure and the intellectual restlessness in his writing, his postulate of self-transcendence through heroic effort, devotion, and sacrifice, as well as his longing for death, which became increasingly deep and pervasive toward the end of his life. Saint-Exupéry yearned for a mystic fusion with his mother's world, which was full of mysterious allure but could not be reached in this life. Death was a literally utopian solution to all problems, enabling the Little Prince to return to the planet of the rose. But to make these connections clear we'll have to take a closer look at Saint-Exupéry's biography and complete *oeuvre*, where flight from the mother constitutes the submerged central motif.

Saint-Exupéry has gone down in history as the poet of flight, and rightly so. Flying wasn't a job, a nine-to-five career, but a lifelong need. Flying saved him from his worst fits of depression.[4] It was the perfect answer to his longing for commitment, for real action. It gave him the much-desired contact with comrades who, like him, were presumably bound to each other by their service.[5] In all Saint-Exupéry's relationships flying meant the masculine world over against his mother. The Little Prince in him, otherwise in danger of remaining an eternal mama's boy because of all his guilt feelings and attachments, strove desperately all his life to demonstrate his independence and masculinity as a flyer.

The struggle against being spoiled by his mother, the search for a boost to his male ego, the longing for camaraderie, the desire for emphatically hard, demanding, "real" tasks often reached an altogether masochistic level. Saint-Exupéry admits this in one of his war letters: "Above all I've longed for everything I had no longing for. For dirt and rain. For attacks of rheumatism on the farm. For unfilled evenings. For melancholy, which is connected with all this unrest ten thousand meters up in the air. Also for fear. That goes without saying, for everything that is demanded of men. And I did that to be a man with men and to come to life with my fellows, because when I part from them, I'm no longer good for anything. I'm so full of contempt for the observers: for the people who in everything they do never dare to commit themselves."[6]

There could be no clearer way of expressing the wish finally to escape the ghetto of the spoiled outsider, and to be among equals. The "men" are those who don't vegetate away in the artificial world of hollow enjoyment and empty witticisms. Life demands from them "deeds" and "sacrifices." Saint-Exupéry takes it for granted that the realm of the "real" and the "human" is identical to a strenuous existence full of sacrifices. He does so, obviously, because in his experience motherly coddling, threats to his masculinity, and latent self-hatred were all one. Saint-Exupéry despises and rejects the "simple," contemplative, theoretical life, which under different circumstances would be a commendable ideal, because it threatened to let him rot. This only heightened his longing to find a replacement for his mother's conflict-ridden love; and he searched for it among his "comrades," a group of men who were bound together by a common task instead of a mother's choking arms.

We know from Saint-Exupéry's biography that his longing for friends and comrades remained in fact an unreached and probably unreachable goal. It derived from the needs expressed in his flight from the rose, rather than from real experiences of human intimacy. There are men whose childhood relations with their mother permanently distort their intelligence and sensibility with an unconscious fear of women.[7] Like all such persons, Saint-Exupéry felt in his own sensitive, aesthetic, reflective nature a temptation, so to speak, or an uncanny envelopment. And he applied all his energy to escape his mother's world through "masculine" ideals that were her polar opposites. In expending this effort he found his true friends.

Friedrich Nietzsche, for whom Saint-Exupéry had a deep affection, resembled him in his escape from the "matriarchy" of his childhood by a flight into the fantasy of the "superman" and the philosophy of great "deed."[8] Saint-Exupéry's contemporary Jean-Paul Sartre sought to escape the maternal prison by postulating absolute freedom, even as he defined human existence as a "useless passion" to create a godlike autonomy, in and for oneself.[9] Above all, Sartre's hatred of the bourgeoisie, his doomed attempt to belong to the "proletarians" (e.g., the Renault workers[10]), and his constant dissatisfaction with himself betray a motivation, method, and goal extraordinarily similar to Saint-Exupéry's futile search for comrades and "real" people.

Saint-Exupéry spent his whole life fleeing from his mother, although in far less revolutionary fashion than Nietzsche or Sartre. His anxiety and guilt toward his mother stifled in him any desire to rebel, while his unlimited respect and reverence for his mother prevented him from challenging, even remotely, the ideals and values she stood for. The conflict between his wistful, regressive tendencies and his anxiety-laden forward strivings drove him to a symbolic mediating expression, which he found in his passionate need to "fly." His biographers are all agreed that Saint-Exupéry's desire to fly could at times become an obsession,[11] often refusing to acknowledge the laws and limits of aerodynamics. There is a lot of evidence suggesting that this obsession with flight is based on the symbolism of the flying dream[12]: on the temptation to escape in a fantastic way from mother earth and gravity, in the notion of boundless independence and freedom from all fetters and confinement, in the feeling of a towering superiority and godlike omnipotence, in the intoxication of adventure, virility, and coming through in the clutch, in a mystical fusion with the universe, in hopes of performing a great deed to give meaning to his life.

One could always argue that elevation in space has nothing per se to do with greatness of soul or personal maturity, but that objection to Saint-Exupéry's passion for flying has little relevance here. "Flying" is in itself an archetypal symbol, a universal human dream that brings to life all the yearnings of the *spirit,* that evokes the lifting of humans high above nature. Thus the Aztec myths of the plumed serpent, in which mind overcomes matter, and what is earthly rises up to heaven under the power of the wind god.[13] Thus all the fairy tales and sagas of all peoples repeatedly telling how a human is transformed into a bird to escape certain forms of dependency.[14] The claim to freedom, intelligence, and power is always concentrated in the symbol of the divine bird or birdman. This is a typical mode of countering de facto dependency, emotional entanglement, and strong self-doubt. It's also the psychic world of Saint-Exupéry's flyer.

Yet even in a plane Saint-Exupéry can't escape the maternal "earth serpent." Every symbol confirms what it negates, and at once means what it denies. The plane itself is a symbol of the mother. Saint-Exupéry was quite clear about the maternal qualities of flying. This can be seen in a passage from *Flight to Arras* where, sitting in the cockpit, he feels like a little child on (or in) his mother's body: "All that tangle of tubes and wiring has become a circulatory network. I am an organism integrated into the plane. I turn this switch, which gradually heats up my overall and my oxygen, and the plane begins to generate my comfort. . . . The plane is my wet-nurse. Before we took off, this thought seemed to me inhuman, but now, suckled by the plane itself, I feel a sort of filial affection for it. The affection of a nursling."[15]

Saint-Exupéry goes a step further when he draws a detailed comparison between a flyer's oxygen intake and a baby's nursing: "From time to time you just pinch with your finger tips a little rubber hose that leads into the mask, to check that it's still under pressure, that there's still milk in the bottle. And then you suck nicely on it."[16]

Much as Saint-Exupéry tries to "fly away" from his mother, he still remains internally connected to her. And this conflict between binding and loosing, dependence and independence, feeling secure and breaking away, forms the latent psychological background of all his thinking. We could call it one long high-altitude flight both from and back to the mother. As with Nietzsche and Sartre, though less consistently, happiness is replaced by the deed, the goal is replaced by the path, being by action, reason by will.[17]

A casual reading of *The Little Prince* will not make most readers aware of how much reflective philosophy Saint-Exupéry has packed into the lessons taught by the fox and the Little Prince himself. You have to read the relevant passages against the background, primarily, of *Citadelle,* as if under a magnifying glass. This is the only way to grasp how radically serious Saint-Exupéry was in demanding from himself strenuous effort, a constant struggle to transcend himself and his own regressive tendencies. Thus he has the "ruler" of the citadel say:

"And the great struggle against things: the hour has come to speak to you about your great error. . . . I have seen those people unhappy, surly, and divided who, though in their luxury they had gotten diamonds, had nothing for sale but worthless stuff made of glass. What you need is not a thing, but a god. . . . For the only purpose of a thing is to make you grow, and you grow only by conquering it but not by possessing it." "The man who toils away hacking at the rock, and once a year burns up the fruit of his work for the glow of light he gets from it, is richer than he who gets fruits every day that come from somewhere else and cost him no labor."[18]

We can clearly sense how earnestly Saint-Exupéry is trying to battle his own spoiled upbringing, the mama's-boy coddling, with all the weapons of his will and a lethal self-contempt. Everything he has been given gratis from his mother strikes him as devalued; and the consumerist happiness that he attacks as the main evil of his time, the destruction of all values through the "anti-thirst pill sellers,"[19] prompts Saint-Exupéry's withering rage. This would scarcely have happened unless these things presented a recurring danger that he had sensed deep down inside himself: that everything given to him in his mother's stifling "goodness" has basically been taken away, because it's been devalued, inflated, and robbed of its meaning. For Saint-Exupéry, the only things that contain meaning, possess greatness, and make us richer are the things that we've personally thirsted for, that we've conquered with our own strenuous effort. This strange idea of Saint-Exupéry's becomes evident only when we think our way into the sphere of his experience, with its background of stifling solicitude and anxious motherly love. This so thoroughly dominates Saint-Exupéry's thinking that he can launch into apodictic generalizations such as the following: "the meaning of things lies not in the already accumulated supply that the sedentary consume, but in the glow of transformation, of the march, or of desire."[20]

The impulse to such an absolutizing of his (intrinsically

more than justified) critique of the "enjoyers," the people rotting away amid the comforts of consumerism, is based not so much on the experiences of a rising mass culture as on the impressions Saint-Exupéry got from his mother's love, a love that provided everything and thereby swallowed it all up. Reacting to that, he took refuge in the ideal of his missing father, the world of masculine "challenge."[21] Love itself seemed dangerous to Saint-Exupéry when and because it turned out to be mere taking possession of someone. Once again the overtones of an only too justified critique of the forms of bourgeois marriage blend with the shrill undertones of Oedipal fear of being enslaved by a love with an undeniable sadistic component, as Saint-Exupéry has his "ruler" say about the citadel: "Your love is based on hatred because you stop short in the man or woman on whom you stock up and whom you begin to hate, like dogs when they swarm around their feeding trough, whoever casts a sidelong glance at your repast. You call your greedy egoism love. The free gift of love is scarcely granted you when, as in your false friendships, you turn it into servitude and slavery and, from the moment you are loved, you begin to discover that you have been injured. And to inflict on others, all the better to enslave them, the spectacle of your suffering. To be sure, you *are* suffering; and it is this very suffering that I dislike; and how can you expect me to admire it?"[22]

If we take him at his word, we see reflected here the sheer anxiety over having to "receive" something or to be given a gift: This is overt fear of his own neediness. And here is where the valid part of Saint-Exupéry's views loses some of its humanity, owing to anxiety-driven exaggerations and generalizations. It's true that love can wreak havoc only if it lays unconditional claims on people and swallows them like a meal. Nevertheless there's no denying that love also consists in having an unconditional need for the other like one's daily bread, because of one's own limitedness and incompleteness. But Saint-Exupéry on principle refused to acknowledge the fact that love might actually have something to do with dependence, connectedness, and reciprocal need. In every passage dealing with this mutual neediness of love, he couldn't help seeing a caricature of primitive egotism, a purely demanding mentality, and parasitical laziness. This looks like the old guilt feelings over having once in his childhood really "used" his mother for his own interests, as well as intense fear of the dreadful state, "pregnant with rot," of a person who had always been coddled and cared for. Against this background of anxiety, Saint-Exupéry, like Nietzsche, found even the Christian ideal of loving and forgiving one's neighbor a dangerous one, because it was soft and decadent.

"First of all, you shall not teach forgiveness and love of neighbor. For they could be misunderstood as meaning only respect for an injury or an ulcer. Rather you shall teach the wonderful collaboration of everyone that is carried out on all, through all, and through each individual."[23]

In this way, by his one-sided opposition of giving to taking, of offering presents to accepting them, Saint-Exupéry inevitably runs the risk of reducing love to nothing but a conceptual goal, a mere utopia. For the lover the beloved is like the air he breathes, like the sea that bears him up, like the light that warms him. Whoever destroys love's neediness destroys its cycle, which consists in a continual exchange of seeking and finding, hope and fulfillment, passion and task. Love lives on inner orientation, which needs the beloved to complete his own nature. Saint-Exupéry, however. is afraid of surfeit from a certain kind of stifling love, and hence he lays so much stress on sacrifice and commitment to the other's happiness that it amounts to an almost autonomous self-giving, a sunlike pouring oneself out in all directions. This one-sidedly activist accent on all human relations finally goes so far that Saint-Exupéry can have the ruler in *Citadelle* proclaim in all sincerity, "I told you, regret for love is love."[24]

For anyone who tries to live with this mentality, that kind of maxim means simply replacing the experience of happiness in love with a demand for continual exertion. To be sure the fox in *The Little Prince* has a point when he says: "It is the time that you have wasted for your rose that makes your rose so important."[25] But in its insistent radicality Saint-Exupéry's standpoint evidently confuses cause with effect: The value of the rose doesn't depend on the sum of the trouble and sacrifices one has expended for the other. On the contrary, so long as a person really loves another, no sacrifice and no trouble seem too great. Of course, you can't learn your true value until you are loved, but really to love, you absolutely have to see and feel your love "with the heart." To the five thousand roses out in the field the Little Prince can rightly say: "You are beautiful, but you are empty."[26]

But if we apply this metaphorical language to the world of human love, it becomes false. In speaking of humans it's offensive to separate outer and inner, beauty and mind, "charm and dignity."[27] And it borders dangerously on contempt or, what comes down to the same thing, the sheer overcompensation of certain impotence fantasies, when you force yourself into the role of a man who could and must fill up a woman, like an empty vessel, with value and substance simply through your own strenuous efforts. The decisive thing in love is not to enrich the other with meaning through a quantum of your own energy. Love is found rather in the art of sensing the absolute value of the other and helping him or her to unfold.

Only in this way can we have the paradisiacal feeling of gratitude that the other exists. *We* don't have to lend the other substance and meaning. The whole world acquires its center, its magnetic field of force, its meaning-creating perspective through the beauty, the magic, and the infinite scope of the beloved. Even the art of "taming" would have to end in monotony, if the soul of the beloved were not like an ocean that with every high tide casts anew the rarest seashells up on the beach, whose waves tell of the most precious pearls and never-seen corals in unfathomable depths of the sea. The discovery of this infinite mystery, the spreading of the soul out into an oceanic feeling of unity in love and eternity, is the only true form of longing in love, and it is obviously the opposite of Saint-Exupéry's melancholy utopia.

For Saint-Exupéry the problem of love, defined as labor, stamina, or responsibility, and rooted in disappointment with human inadequacy, had to extend to the experience of all things. As Saint-Exupéry sees it, nothing, no structure in space, no ceremony in time, possesses a pre-established value. That's why he was so keen on stamping meaning and value on lifeless "stuff" through ascetical voluntarism. The freedom to find meaning in love thus had to be distorted into the compulsion to constitute meaning in action and sacrifice.[28] Thus the "Father-Chief" explains: "And my constraint is there to help you. And I compel my priests to offer sacrifice, even when their sacrifices no longer make any sense [sic!]. I compel my sculptors to sculpt, even when they have doubts about themselves. I compel my sentries to take their hundred steps under pain of death. Otherwise they are already dead, killed by themselves, and cut off by themselves from the empire. I save them by my harshness."[29]

In all his thought and emotions, with all his humanity and inimitable *noblesse,* Saint-Exupéry seems light-years away from the atrocities of fascism. But this "philosophy" of voluntarism, with its violent Promethean compulsion, leads him in a highly disquieting fashion right into the danger of fascist ideology. It is just this sort of tragic air of struggle and failure that we find in Nietzsche's motto, "Am I looking for happiness? I am looking for my work!"[30] It is this pathos of an activist and voluntarist ideology, which supposedly creates meaning and value, that in the final analysis reduces all things, all people, every individual to the level of raw material, to mere building blocks of cyclopean masonry.

In *Night Flight,* which articulates the total ambivalence of Saint-Exupéry's thinking, Rivière, for example, is thoroughly aware that the ambitious decision to open up the Patagonia airmail line may call for considerable sacrifices in human life, leading to a head-on collision with the interests and the rights of women and children to their husbands and fathers.[31] But what's the use of this abstract recognition of the rights of women and children, when they're stacked against the claims of grown men? There may be genuine tragic conflicts where your responsibilities force you to do things that you can absolutely never take responsibility for, things for which you can only ask forgiveness.[32] But tragedies of this sort arise out of a moral dialectic, not, as with Saint-Exupéry, out of a metaphysical dualism of the sexes — that is, unless we apply the label of tragic to the ambivalence that continually drags him into anxious contradictions as he strives to be both masculine and human.

Only when "masculinity" is perceived to be no more than a hasty antagonism to the supposedly protective, preserving, nondynamic attitude of femininity, can we grasp the "masculine protest" implied in seeing the man's task as giving birth to himself through the contrary attitudes of action, rebellion, and struggle. Ultimately *Night Flight* no longer cares about the goals for which human beings are being sacrificed to realize:

"Victory, defeat — the words were meaningless. Life lies behind these symbols and life is ever bringing new symbols into being. One nation is weakened by victory, another finds new forces in defeat. Tonight's defeat conveyed perhaps a lesson which would speed the coming of final victory. The work in progress was all that mattered."[33]

This sort of historical dynamism can justify literally anything, including the Nazi mystique. If the movement of history needs sacrificial victims to create itself in the ups and downs of victory and defeat, we can no longer avoid an ideology of history, as seen most graphically in the Aztecs' bloody rituals: The "Fourth World," produced by the conflicts between earth and air, fire and water — primeval symbols of the opposition between male and female — maintains its forward momentum only by slaughtering people, whose flesh serves to nurture the gods.[34] Once such a lapse back into the mythology of history is accepted, any kind of barbarism becomes possible if not necessary.

In point of fact, the mystique of blood and sacrifice justifies nothing; and the hecatombs that the gods need for their own self-preservation don't make them worthy of veneration, only more repulsive. But to leave behind the world of such mystifications, the first requirement is that the experience of love, the mystery of woman, be liberated from its frightening obsessions – without losing its magical fascination. And so the crucial question becomes, how is it possible to grasp, deep down, the feminine and maternal principle – as a place of nondevouring security, as an abode of eternal life? In the final analysis the question is, what God, what *image* of God do you believe in?

Unlike Nietzsche, unlike Sartre, who openly attacked Christian faith in the Godman, countering it with the image of the superman, the human god, Saint-Exupéry diffidently and piously picks up the conventional term "God" in his work. But he does so while holding on to everything in the old religion that struck him as either hollow or holy, filling it with often completely contradictory contents. Ultimately this brings him much closer to the atheism of Nietzsche and Sartre than to the biblical image of God, and this new conception of the image of God basically feeds on his anxiety of being choked to death in the arms of a "motherly" God.

When Saint-Exupéry speaks of "God," he generally means a principle of human self-transcendence, a reaching beyond oneself, a rejection of human consolation – a concentration of unrest within, a mountaintop crucifix without, on the other side of the mountains that must be climbed. He vehemently resists connecting human notions, even the biblical ones, of God as a "person," as "goodness," as a "father," with this absolute Beyond. He believes – rightly – that the reasons for modern atheism are to be sought in, among other places, the humanization of the concept of God (or as Nietzsche would have put it, in the philosophy of the "sheep").[35] But this protest against the false consolations of the Christian image of God leads

Saint-Exupéry to abandon the hopes of Christianity one and all. He has his "ruler" say:

"For you are accustomed to wish, if you doubt God, that God should show himself to you like someone who comes strolling along to pay you a visit. But then whom would you be meeting except an equal, someone like yourself, who would lead you nowhere and thus lock you into your loneliness? For you don't long for the revelation of the God's majesty, just a spectacle and fairground festival. And so all you would get would be a vulgar fairground pleasure – and a sense of bristling disappointment with God. And how could you display so much vulgarity? But you want something to come down to you, to visit you, as you are, on your level, and humble itself before you, and without reason, so you will never be heard as I was in my search for God. On the contrary, the spiritual realms will open up and the apparitions will dazzle you, being meant neither for the eyes nor for the understanding but for the heart and spirit, if you strive to climb up and if you reach the level where we no longer find things, but the divine knots that link them together."[36]

One could not image a crasser contradiction of the Christian notion of God's "revelation" to humanity or God's "incarnation" in a human being. For Saint-Exupéry there is no God who comes to the person, to have compassion on human distress amid a world full of fear and helplessness. There is only the possibility of ascending to "God." In the language of the ruler: "If I want...to teach God to you I would first send you mountain climbing, so that the starlit crest could tempt you to the full. I would make you die of thirst in the desert, so that the wells could send you into transports. Then I would send you for six months to split rocks, so that the noonday sun annihilated you. Then

I would tell you: The man who has drunk up the noonday sun, who has climbed the starry crest, will slake his thirst in the silence of the divine wells, once the mystery of the night draws near. And thus you will believe in God."[37]

For Saint-Exupéry "God" — or belief in "God" — arises only out of the experience of what the individual exacts from himself or herself. And since all things reveal their value only through human commitment and sacrifice, "God" too can be nothing but the quintessence of reality that a person finds in self-denial. This "God" doesn't answer a single human question but rather is just a principle for challenging every kind of human self-assurance and self-satisfaction. In a sense this God is like the Kaaba in Mecca, though of course minus the angel Gabriel and his messages to the prophet Muhammad: This God is a black rock that would be nothing without the touch of many hands, without the sweat of foreheads, without the prayers of pilgrims who have crossed the desert to get there. It's not a place where something could be found but an abode where one can discover that being a pilgrim, the transcending of boundaries, has in itself no boundaries.[38]

Because upon closer inspection this "transcendence," this "pilgrimage" is not aimed at a reachable goal. Rather, Saint-Exupéry's restless transcendence is, like Sartre's, merely a flight from the feeling of one's own nothingness, and hence a path into total isolation from God as well as from all men and women. "O Lord, at times my loneliness is icy," even the ruler has to confess, "and I yearn for a sign in the wilderness of my abandonment. But in the course of a dream you have taught me. I have realized that all signs are vain. Because if you were on my level, then you wouldn't force me to grow. And what can I do with myself, O Lord, the way I am now?"[39]

In Saint-Exupéry's work, this shame at one's own "little-ness," this constant dissatisfaction with oneself, this fear of one's own "unmanliness," this "castration complex," to borrow a Freudian term, admittedly veils itself in a quasi-religious language. In other words, it's a language that believes in nothing, so it can create everything, and that refuses to be comforted by anything found in order to find its greatness in the "takeoff." And yet it would be misreading Saint-Exupéry to fail at the same time to see the opposite positions in all these statements, which are enormously exaggerated and often can be understood only as antitheses. Prompted by fear and self-contempt, Saint-Exupéry continually and consistently rejected the assumption that the world had a "maternal" background. Yet this same man was nevertheless practically enchanted by nostalgic memories of his mother's world. Saint-Exupéry suffered deeply from the destruction of the traditional values of his childhood, and his basic bent was thoroughly conservative.

We can have no comprehension of Saint-Exupéry's life and work, and least of all his discussions about "God," unless we note this continual contradiction: He denied most vehemently what he most longed for, and he longed most of all for what he first sought to fly farthest from. The same Saint-Exupéry who sees God as, at best, the embodiment of the principle of ceaseless self-transcendence, of chronic existential unrest, can also unhesitatingly declare — in the same passage — that God is the guarantor of eternity. First he demands that people go on climbing and climbing, in a permanent upward pilgrimage. Then he immediately proceeds to describe "God" as humanity's hearth and home. Scarcely has he finished praising the absolute value of action, sacrifice, commitment, etc., and pronouncing that the dynamic of history is the last word on all questions, than he is seized by a desire for something solid and lasting. It sounds like a fundamental confession of all his other contrary convictions when he has his ruler say:

"I, God's servant, thirst after eternity. I hate everything that changes. I strangle the man who rises at night and casts his prophecies to the winds, like a tree struck by a lightning flash by the seed from heaven, when it cracks and burns the forest with it. When God moves, I am terrified; let him, the Immutable one, stay put in Eternity! There is a time for genesis, but there is a time, a blessed time, for custom. We must pacify and fructify and polish. I am the one who sews up the clefts in the ground, and I hide from men the traces of the volcano. I am the lawn on the edge of the abyss.... That is why I protect him who in the seventh generation resumes the job, to take it to perfection.... I love the pregnant woman or the one nursing her child, I love the flock that perpetuates itself, I love the returning seasons. For, first of all, I am the one who dwells. O Citadel, my dwelling, I will save you from the plotting of the sands. I will adorn you with bugles, to sound against the barbarians."[40]

Now at a stroke the "nomads" and "homeless," whom the ruler has just praised as the gypsies of existence, are labeled "barbarians." All of a sudden what matters is now holding on to what you have, now striking camp and moving on – because fear of the abyss is threatening.

Contradictions like these are familiar to us, for example, in the world of Nietzsche. Nietzsche's spiritual kinship with Saint-Exupéry repeatedly catches the reader's eye; and it evidently derives from the same source, fear of woman. Nietzsche too first brands any notion of eternal duration as a Platonic-Christian falsification of history and the world. And then he looks to cyclical thinking, to the idea of the eternal return, trying to get as close as possible to the concept of being.[41] Similarly Saint-Exupéry makes it clear how much he wants back the world that he was so eager to escape. In fact the dynamism of his worldview basically stems from disappointed traditionalism. Whereas Nietzsche forced himself to accept "homelessness" and to climb to increasingly greater heights of loneliness,[42] Saint-Exupéry never stopped yearning for what he had lost.

At the apogee of the spiritual challenge laid down when Nietzsche's "supermen" were in the process of turning all of Europe into their Valhalla,[43] Saint-Exupéry had only one solution for the disasters of his day: to *mourn* the destruction of all the values of his childhood, but with no prospect of salvation. He had nothing left but a powerful longing for death, the mindset of "Saint Ex," as his comrades jokingly called him; and he openly confessed in his "Letter to a General": "It's all the same to me if I die in the war. What will be left, then, of what I loved? I'm not speaking simply of the people, but also of the customs, of the irreplaceable accents, of a certain spiritual light.... The things that remain intact are a matter of complete indifference to me. The crucial point is a certain arrangement of things. Culture is an invisible good, since it isn't concerned with things, but with the invisible bonds that join things together: this way and not otherwise. Big sets of musical instruments can be handed out to us, but where will the musicians be? If I should die in the war, I don't much care.... Still, if I do return home from this 'necessary and thankless job,' then I'll be faced with a problem: what are we to say to the people?"[44]

At the end of his life Saint-Exupéry tried to resolve this most crucial of all questions with a double answer. But at bottom it really just restated the central conflict of his life rather than enabling him to overcome it: The Little Prince returns to his rose while the crashed flyer takes off again, a conclusion that doesn't conclude, a finale that finally clarifies nothing. This time, once and for all, Saint-Exupéry's regressive and progressive tendencies come to a parting of the ways, unreconciled and unmediated. There was a chance that in the looming catastrophe the Little Prince and the flyer might have been fused into a living unity, but that has now gone forever by the board. Instead, the dynamic of the Oedipus complex, so to speak, won a victory: the return to the world of the mother and, as the inevitable price for that, death. In the face of a world coming apart at the seams Saint-Exupéry longed for his childhood. We have to take quite literally the wish he expressed in his last letter to his mother, which I cited earlier: He wanted nothing more than to return to his mother's arms and to play the role of the Little Prince by her side. He would prefer to be her big boy, without the "stupidities" of his boyhood — the sheep had to keep its muzzle on. And now, after many years, he would be old enough to do justice to the rose and admit she was right.

It would be a wonderful dream, and nevertheless a wish that amounted to definitive resignation and capitulation. Once again Saint-Exupéry was proud enough to take up for the last time the struggle for his adult masculinity. This is also the direction we have to look in interpreting the death of the Little Prince: Saint-Exupéry finally tried to repress his longing to go back. Instead of incorporating the figure of the "child," he plunged once and for all into the realm of utopia. Still, he didn't fail to ask his readers to show him a way out, should they ever meet the Little Prince. This was a clear cry for help, though it comes too late. On this earth the only one we'll get to know is the flyer. The Little Prince is dead; long live the "ruler" of *Citadelle.*[45] But this is a heartbreaking dichotomy that raises more questions than it settles.

Chapter 7

Between the Wisdom of the Sands and the Heavenly Jerusalem

ભ

WE HAVE EXPLORED *The Little Prince* in order to find out to what extent we can read the twentieth century's most important fairy tale as a dream that heals the splits in our consciousness, as a path that leads out of the mind's darkness into light, and as a place where the soul can rediscover itself. The results of this exploration give us little grounds for hope or confidence.

In comparison with Franz Kafka's anti-fairy tales Saint-Exupéry's work no doubt resembles an oasis in the desert, and measured against the cold, snowbound lostness of *The Castle, Citadelle* is like a blooming garden. Its world-view offers accurate criticism, grand perspectives, and a prophetically radical way of asking questions. In addition it is presented with the infectious charm of expressive eloquence. The book is animated above all by the consciousness of values that must be rescued if humanity is to survive. It strives to shore up the shaky foundations of the human world through the witness and commitment of the individual. A person could hardly do more — and yet Saint-Exupéry's work is lacking a decisive element: the power of synthesis.

From a philosophical standpoint, Saint-Exupéry is incapable of coping with the "metaphysical situation of our time."[1] His aversion to the complexities of "logic" and the entanglements of analytical reason forces him to adopt a kind of intuition based on immediate evidence. This approach refuses to work through the problems actually at hand and to provide argumentative support for the proposed solutions. No doubt it offers quite a few high-altitude "aerial photos," but that's no substitute for digging down into the territory "on the ground."

For all its poetic and symbolic evocativeness Saint-Exupéry's thinking remains basically abstract and proves powerless to interpret historical reality in a meaningful way. Meanwhile his flight from concreteness, his fear of being touched by reality, his reduction of spiritual synthesis to mere argumentation is not caused by some lack of logical consistency. Rather it arises out of a profound ambivalence: From the *psychological* standpoint, Saint-Exupéry won't let himself reach his goal. He has learned to fear what he loves. He has to *avoid* what could give him rest and support. And again conversely he has to affirm what denies him, seek what threatens him, and deny what he most longs for. This amounts to a struggle with no pauses to catch one's breath, a heroic myth, in which the boa constrictor of childhood is changed into the death-bearing redemptress of maturity.

In this ambivalent state everything that ought to form a psychic unity disintegrates into a sad melancholy made up of childlike love and tenderness and a Promethean formation of a self marked by "masculine" toughness and isolation. With a last desperate effort Saint-Exupéry counters the spreading human desert with the mentality of compulsion, with value-creating will, the demand of action against the world of happiness. But does the ruler (Saint-Exupéry's original title for the book was *Le Caïd*) succeed in protecting his walls against time's destructive hand? Does his "citadel" hold out against the penetration of the desert?

Saint-Exupéry's great concern was to overcome the nihilism of our time through the power of a transcendent vision, by a demanding architecture of human life. His work must be measured against this goal; any other standard would be beneath someone of his stature. But then we have to say that there can be no meaningful transcendence of human existence, so long as the background of the world, the underworld of existence, remains so grossly distorted by fear, as it is in Saint-Exupéry's art and experience.

The crucial question is *not* how can people fight against the experience of their nothingness, against the self-hatred of pure meaninglessness, against the shapelessness of the dust, by striving with all their might and main to fashion for themselves a self-portrait, a solid structure, a certain amount of value and dignity. The question is rather how are people to overcome their fear of nothingness through a deeper trust in the justification of their existence, and how they are to find their way back to the peaceful measure of their existence. The authentic human person is not created by the ascetical terror of duty, action, responsibility, and sacrifice. On the contrary, the ideology of the superman, of the man-god, of Daedalus, has been proved more hopelessly wrong in this century than in any other. No kind of compulsion and violence can save us from self-hatred and revulsion, and they can never liberate us from the latent cynicism of all Promethean attempts to bring forth a newer, supposedly better, greater person from ourself and others.

In principle this is the only really decisive question of human existence: How can we relieve the anxiety over being nothing more than, as the Bible says, "dust" (Gen. 3:19)?[2] So long as we have to fear the hands that shaped the clay, have to fear them as something choking and constricting, we will invest all our powers in getting free of those hands. We will press to the outermost limit our flight from the threatened dependence and therefore impose on ourselves the demand of drawing our own self-image. Fearing distortion by strangers and hating ourselves for being spineless, amorphous Silly Putty, we are driven by an overload of stress into squeezing the worthless coal dust of existence into a precious diamond.

But the example of Saint-Exupéry can serve as a proof of the inescapable dilemma posed by this attempt: In the background the yearning will only get stronger for a smaller, more protected, less exhausting world, where it would be enough simply to exist. And the world of the "child" and the world of the "grown-up" will spin further and further apart, severing even more thoroughly the longing to be allowed to exist from the insistent need to give shape to things, the wish to be accepted in our smallness from the demand to "do our own thing" and so reach greatness.

In this vicious circle of longing and struggle, of taking off to the mothers and taking off to the stars, there is only one way out: being satisfied with believing what the Bible says on its very first page about the creation of the human race ("in the beginning God formed the dust of the earth and breathed life into it," Gen. 2:7). We have nothing to fear from this maternal "shaping" background of the world. Instead, the force that molds our essence is at the same time the one that bears us up, what molds us holds us, what tests our hearts preserves them too. Our task is not to overcome the human element; it's simply to discover it. The "ruler" can never redeem the "desert" and halt its spreading devastation. Only the Little Prince could do that, provided he's liberated from the Oedipal inclination to incest, from homosexuality, macho delusions, and the castration complex.

Because there is truth in the religious legacy we find condensed in the figure of the Little Prince, and Saint-Exupéry was very close to this truth: In every single person the face of God waits for its appearance.[3] In every single person we must find God's work of art. Every single person, whether Leonardo, Mozart, Shakespeare, or you and I, bears deep within himself or herself an image, a music, a word of eternity that can be spoken, expressed, sketched out only in him or her. We must dive down to the bottom of this eternal and indestructible element, which shines forth in the eyes of the beloved like the stars in the heavens on the clear mirror of a calm sea.

The garden of the human world blossoms most beautifully not through "action," "strenuousness," "force," "will" — like Michelangelo working on a block of marble. What makes our world blossom is rather the art of patient watching, thoughtful listening, tender union, and the involuntary harmony of the heart. So the key point is not to form and shape it, but to let it ripen and lift it to the light.

There is such an endless number of things to discover in a person whom one loves, things that can be seen only with the eyes of love. And this reverent gratitude for the existence of the beloved transforms every moment with him or her into a temple of devotion and prayer. People are joined together not by "jobs," or "sweating together." What binds them forever is this harmony of the soul, this trembling wave of happiness, this quivering billow of joy, that bears them irresistibly up to the sky. One need not want to build a "ship" or erect a "temple,"[4] to establish the value of a person. It's the other way around: you enter the soul of the beloved as if it were a shrine, since you are now close to God. You sense in her affection how warmly the light of divinity floods through the high windows. And it seems as if the gates wanted to swing open now to the shore of eternity, as if, as the Egyptians believed,[5] the bark of the sun lay on the shore ready to depart. And one need only let oneself be borne on the waves of love across to what we call the "other world" and the "beyond," because there beyond space and time the hearts of lovers fuse together forever, where, unlike here, they can, and must, be united forever, bonded forever.

Ultimately you have to choose here between the vision of *Citadelle* and the biblical vision of the heavenly Jerusalem. The walls and ruins of the "city in the desert" are built on the shifting sands of history. Their towers defiantly thrust out against the transitoriness of the dust. The burning desert wind swirls through the streets, and its hot breath burns the hearts and mouths of people with thirst. As if in a forge their form melts until it gradually changes into a new shape and fullness. What they are "worth" comes from their "exchange value." Though nothing in themselves, they are parts of the "knot," building blocks of the pyramid, a decoration on the shrine. In this context loving a person means creating that person, through the compulsion of privation and sacrifice, first and fore-most as a human being, and refashioning that person into a member of the "kingdom."

In contrast to all this, the ancient Egyptians along the great oasis of the Nile, fifteen hundred years before the first biblical texts, looked up to heaven. And when they did, they saw in the host of stars a reflection of their little world, only this time exalted into infinity and eternity. Once again the huts and palaces of the earthly Old Cairo stretched out across the firmament, as if they wanted to sport about like a jewel on the nightgown of the heavenly goddess Nut. Once again there arose on the Mountains of the Heart, east of Cairo, the companions of the Night, the baboon-headed children of the moon god Thot, greeting the sight of the newborn son with their howling benediction.[6] Once again on the shores of the heavenly Nile the maids went to the well, the deal-ers to market, the children to school, and over all this spread the infinite worthiness, the eternal meaning, and the everlasting beauty of light: On one and all rested the promise of eternity, for everything on earth was just a mirror of heaven, a prelude to happiness. And the magic of love was already bridging the distance, even then, between there and beyond, between death and immortality.

By picking up and confirming these images in the vision of the New Jerusalem, the New Testament also gives Chris-tianity the same religious orientation: "And I saw the holy city, new Jerusalem, coming down out of heaven from God, prepared as a bride, adorned for her husband" (Rev. 21:2). Granted, these images paint our hope only in reflections from this world. But in love it is still possible to discover the earthly as a promise of our eternal home. If we're fortunate, we will never have to take heaven by storm. But in the happiness of love heaven appears to be already swooping down to earth and swathing with its blessing everything that joins lovers. When the whole world begins to sing and is transfigured in the chorus of tenderness, then a little piece of earth has already been transformed into a piece of heaven. And if we, mortal as we are, still find every word of love unforgettable, shouldn't love itself be proof of the immortality of the person we love? If the world is transformed into a deathless song of love, then we sense that God begins to speak: "And I heard a loud voice from the throne, saying, 'Behold the dwelling of God is with men' " (Rev. 21:3).

We shall not be able to see God with the eyes of our earthly nature, but we will sense God as the power of love in our own hearts and, exactly as on earth, we will recognize God in the eyes of our beloved. For we will see one another again. Love, which is God, has taught us this.

Do we find an answer here to the challenge of our century? Not automatically, to be sure. But only from this source can our thinking be stabilized into a unity that gives us a more integral vision of things. Perhaps toward the end of our lives we'll be asked what we've done to alleviate the distress of our time. And whatever we managed to do, it won't be much. Perhaps we'll be asked how many of our time's leading ideas we have understood, and how many of its errors we have refuted. And we'll have to say that we have remained generations behind the "cutting edge." We have been unsteady in our thinking and helpless in handling the questions put to us. But if asked what was the point of our being on earth to begin with, let's hope we can answer: We strove to see the world with the eyes of love.[7] We rediscovered the Little Prince amid the desert of our own hearts, and in our lives there were eyes that looked upon us like windows into eternity. We have embarked together on the ship that carries us over to the other shore. The ancient Egyptians were right: To the eyes of love the whole world is only the veil, the shimmer, the shadow of eternity.[8]

Notes

ക

The following abbreviations will be used for Saint-Exupéry's most frequently cited works: TLP=*The Little Prince,* trans. Katherine Woods (New York: Harcourt, Brace & World, 1943); CIT=*Citadelle,* in *Oeuvres d'Antoine de Saint-Exupéry* (Paris: Gallimard, 1953). A highly incomplete translation of *Citadelle* is Stuart Gilbert's *The Wisdom of the Sands* (New York: Harcourt, Brace & World, 1950). *Wind, Sand, and Stars, Night Flight,* and *Flight to Arras,* translated by Stuart Gilbert and Lewis Galantière, have been published together as *Airman's Odyssey* (New York: Harcourt, Brace, Jovanovich, 1984), but will be cited respectively as WSS, NF, and FTA.

Introduction

1. CIT, no. 147, 818.
2. I mean something like the end of Shakespeare's *A Midsummer Night's Dream,* V, 1.
3. CIT, no. 35, 781.
4. CIT, no. 78, 693.
5. Franz Kafka, *The Castle,* trans. Willa and Edwin Muir (New York: Schocken, 1988). Curtis Cate contrasts the loneliness in Kafka's Castle with the loneliness of the Little Prince on his planet, which is very closely connected with the experience of a distant God (*Antoine de Saint-Exupéry: His Life and Times* [London: Heinemann, 1970], 457). Thus Saint-Exupéry notes: "Too soon deprived of God at an age when

135

one still seeks refuge, here we must struggle for life like solitary little fellows."

6. On the first introduction to CIT, see Luc Estang, *Saint-Exupéry par lui-même* (Paris: Editions du Seuil, 1948), 67ff. R. M. Albérès rightly calls TLP, "a strange and enchanting book, more moving than fairy tales" — a book that could also serve to show how one should write for "the children of our century" (*Saint-Exupéry,* Bibliothèque de l'Aviation 1 [Paris, 1946], 243). Yves Le Hir rightly points out that Saint-Exupéry concurs with fairy tale models, even in the details (*Fantaisie et mystique dans "Le petit prince" de Saint-Exupéry* [Paris: Nizet, 1954], 22-23). Thus when the king says to the Little Prince, "Approach, so that I may see you better" (35), this is a line that the wolf uses with Little Red Riding Hood; or when the Little Prince says to the vain man, "That is a queer hat you are wearing" (39), he's picking up Little Red Riding Hood's question to the wolf disguised as grandmother.

PART ONE: THE MESSAGE

Chapter 1
The Royal Child — A Quasi-Religious Rediscovery

1. The model for this could be E. T. A. Hoffmann's story, "Das fremde Kind," in *Die Serapionsbrüder* (1819-21), in *Werke in 5 Bänden,* ed. G. Spiekerkötter (Zurich, 1965) 4:222-58.

2. In German the word *böse* (bad, nasty) stems from the root *bhou,* to blow up. On this point as well as on the derivation of evil from anxiety see E. Drewermann, *Strukturen des Bösen,* 2d expanded ed., 3 vols. (Paderborn, 1980), 3:lxxvi-lxxviii.

3. The concept of the "as-if facade" comes from G. Ammon, "Psychodynamik des Suizidgeschehens," in *Handbuch der dynamischen Psychiatrie* (Munich, 1979), 1:779.

4. F. M. Dostoyevsky, *The Idiot,* trans. Eva M. Martin (London: Dent, 1970), pt. 1, chap. 6, 63-73.

5. Georges Bernanos, *Diary of a Country Priest,* trans. Pamela Morris (Chicago: Thomas More Press, 1983), 147-81.

6. The "divine child" is an archetypical image, which as the fruit of a union of opposites (consciousness and the unconscious) is the psychological and theological reflection of the "place" occupied by an existence that has hitherto been unlived but is now awaking to new life.

See K. Kerényi and C. G. Jung, *Das göttliche Kind in mythologischer und psychologischer Beleuchtung* (Amsterdam and Leipzig, 1940). It is worth stressing that even today the Nepalese cult of the Kumari (an incarnation of the divine protectress Taleyu) celebrates and venerates a divine child. See P. Koch and H. Stegmüller, *Geheimnisvolles Nepal: Buddhistische und hinduistische Feste* (Munich, 1983), 103–14.

7. WSS, 205–6. K. Rauch cites this passage in the same sense, but Rauch never asks, any more than Saint-Exupéry's biographers do, to what extent this image of a *destroyed* life has to be applied to Saint-Exupéry himself and his thought ("Antoine de Saint-Exupéry: Mensch und Werk," in *Erinnerungen* [Esslingen, 1958], 51).

Chapter 2
The Grown-ups: Portraits of Loneliness

1. TLP, 27. Y. Le Hir rightly characterizes the "big people" as those who "have lost freshness of heart, spontaneity of impressions and judgments," as people "who are familiar with no order or values except a material one, and in whom the disinterested sense of beauty and poetry has died" (*Fantaisie et mystique dans "Le petit prince,"* 27–28). In this sense the "big people" are not simply the "grown-ups," but the countertype of "children." Both types reflect basic human attitudes.

2. Following the bipartite epistemological scheme in Arthur Schopenhauer, *The World as Will and Idea,* trans. R. B. Haldan and J. Kemp, 3 vols. (London, 1906), vols. 2–3.

3. TLP, 38.

4. Fyodor M. Dostoyevsky correctly observes: "Do you know that there is a limit of ignominy, beyond which man's consciousness of shame cannot go, and after which begins satisfaction in shame?" (*The Idiot,* trans. Eva Martin [London: Dent, 1970], pt. 3, chap. 2, 397).

5. Søren Kierkegaard opposes the desperation of weakness to the desperation of defiance (*Sickness unto Death,* trans. Alistair Hannay [New York: Penguin-Viking, 1985], 49ff). On Kierkegaard's presentation of the concept of despair, see Eugene Drewermann, *Strukturen des Bösen,* 3:287–92.

6. Thus Henrik Ibsen ends *The Wild Duck* with Relling's observation about Hjalmar Ekdal's narcissistic enjoyment of his daughter's death: "Before the year is out, little Hedwig will be no more to him than

a theme on which to exercise his eloquence!" (*Eight Plays by Henrik Ibsen,* trans. Eva Le Gallienne [New York: Modern Library, 1982], 342).

7. This is how Dostoyevsky describes the despair of the hopeless alcoholic Marmeladov in *Crime and Punishment,* trans. David McDuff (London: Viking, 1991), pt. 1, ch. 2, 43–55.

8. On the fetishistic character of addiction see Eugen Drewermann, *Psychoanalyse und Moraltheologie,* vol. 3: *An den Grenzen des Lebens* (Mainz, 1984).

9. Eugen Drewermann, *Der tödliche Fortschritt,* 90–110, describes nature's lack of rights in the Christian-Western world picture.

10. J. Lame Deer and R. Erdoes, *Lame Deer: Seeker of Visions* (New York: Simon and Schuster, 1972), 123.

11. Ibid., 43.

12. Ibid., 44.

13. K. Recheis and G. Bydlinski, *Weisst du, dass die Bäume reden? Weisheit der Indianer* (Vienna, Freiburg, Basel, 1983), 93.

14. E.g., WSS, 135–36, where the author, almost dead from thirst, can still admire the wisdom of the fennec, which never eats all the snails on an individual cactus plant, so as not to endanger the survival of his prey. See Eugen Drewermann, *Der tödliche Fortschritt,* 83–84.

15. TLP, 67.

16. Karl Marx argues concerning the fixing of prices for land: " ... the income, and hence the value of land, ... develops along with the market for the product of the land, and hence with the growth of the non-agricultural population, with their need and their quest for both foodstuffs and raw materials" (*Capital: A Critique of Political Economy,* trans. Charles H. Kerr et al. [Moscow: Progress Publishers, 1971], 3:650).

17. In fairy tales the image for this is the motif of "selling one's soul." See, for example, the Grimms' fairy tale, "The Girl Without Hands" (*Kinder- und Haus Märchen* 31; hereafter abbreviated KHM); Eugen Drewermann and Ingritt Neuhaus, "Das Mädchen ohne Hände," in *Grimms Märchen tiefenpsychologisch gedeutet,* 6 vols. [Olten and Freiburg, 1981–85], 1:31–32.

18. The concept of "real time" (*la durée réelle*) plays a major role in the philosophy of Henri Bergson. See his *Time and Free Will: An Essay on the Immediate Data of Consciousness,* trans. F. L. Pogson (London: G. Allen & Unwin, 1971). Bergson criticizes physics for constructing an ideal scheme of abstract, infinitely divisible time that simply presents the result of fixation and division, and that provides points of departure only in the fixation of becoming (*Matter and Memory,* trans.

Nancy Margaret and W. Scott Palmer [New York: Zone Books, 1988], 234–35). In fact through quantum mechanics physics has overcome the geometrization of time in Einstein's theory of general relativity. On this issue see L. de Broglie, "Die Anschauungen der modernen Physik und der Bergsonschen Begriffe der Zeit," in *Licht und Materie* (Frankfurt, 1958), 2:166–81.

19. The concept of "other-directedness" comes from David Riesman, *The Lonely Crowd* (New Haven: Yale University Press, 1984), 126. Riesman defines the other-directed person as someone who sees the meaning of all activities in coping with other people. "The frontiers for the other-directed man are people; he is people-minded." Riesman contrasts other-directedness to the inner-directed and tradition-directed ways of life.

20. See Stefan Zweig, *Magellan* (Frankfurt: Fischer, 1977), 145ff.

21. See Søren Kierkegaard, *The Present Age,* trans. Alexander Dru (New York: Harper & Row, 1962), 90–92: "The Difficulty of My Task," where Kierkegaard accuses official, "tenured" Christianity as a "criminal case," a "selling of souls," and a "counterfeiting."

22. Nietzsche speaks of the "vanity of the historian," which hides its "banality" and "flatheadedness" in the concept of "objectivity," simply to save itself the work of plunging lovingly and artistically into the empirical data (Friedrich Nietzsche, *Untimely Meditations,* trans. R. J. Hollingdale).

23. CIT, no. 100, 824.

24. Thus Søren Kierkegaard defines faith as trust "for this life" (*Fear and Trembling,* 19). On the concept of faith as a "double movement of the infinite" in Kierkegaard, see Eugen Drewermann, *Strukturen des Bösen,* 3:224.

Chapter 3
The Wisdom of the Desert and the Quest of Love

1. TLP, 58.
2. TLP, 61.
3. Ibid.
4. Saint-Exupéry, "Lettre au Général X," in Jean-Claude Ibert, *Antoine de Saint-Exupéry* (Paris: Éditions Universitaires, 1953), 116.
5. Ibid., 117.
6. Ibid., 118. In fact the image of the human desert is reminiscent of

Friedrich Nietzsche, "Among the Daughters of the Desert": "The deserts grow: woe to him who harbours deserts" (*Thus Spoke Zarathustra*, trans. R. J. Hollingdale [Harmondsworth: Penguin, 1978], pt. 4, 318).

7. Saint-Exupéry, "Lettre au Général X," 120.

8. WSS, 198-99.

9. Thus in the Bible we see Moses, Elijah, John the Baptist, and Jesus in the wilderness preparing themselves for God's truth. Y. Le Hir correctly says that the symbolism of the details in *The Little Prince* is transparent enough, and an "initiation into the spiritual life." The desert "is not just the symbol of a stage in the interior life; in its material reality it is also the privileged framework for encounters with God in silence and solitude" (*Fantaisie et mystique dans "Le petit prince,"* 48-49). Unfortunately Le Hir doesn't proceed to make observations on the other symbols; evidently he is unaware of the psychoanalytical mode of understanding symbols.

10. Qu'ran 5, 4, a text from Muhammad's Medina period, declares "Islam" — "submission to God" — to be religion itself. See L. Gardet, *Connaître Islam* (Paris: Arthème Fayard, 1958), 21.

11. CIT, no. 138, 804.

12. The symbolism for this is the Christian architecture of the baptismal font at the entrance to the church: You enter the sanctuary as if you were climbing down into the world-well, into the western sea, in order to die to superficial views of the world. And then, renewed through the truth of the depths, you return to the world in rejuvenated form. In the fairy tales this motif is most beautifully addressed in the story of "Frau Holle" (KHM 24). See Eugen Drewermann and Ingritt Neuhaus, "Frau Hölle," in *Grimms Märchen tiefenpsychologisch gedeutet* (Olten and Freiburg, 1982), 3:32-35, 50, n. 49.

13. On the symbolism of the snake as the essence of contingency, of the transition between day and night, bright and dark, dry land and sea, consciousness and the unconscious, being and nonbeing see Eugen Drewermann, *Strukturen des Bösen,* 2d expanded ed., 1979, 1:llxv-lxxvi; 2:69-111. On death as nature's final path of grace in hopeless situations see Eugen Drewermann, "Vom Problem des Selbstmords oder: von einer letzten Gnade der Natur," in *Psychoanalyse und Moraltheologie,* vol. 3, *An den Grenzen des Lebens.*

14. See Eugen Drewermann and Ingritt Neuhaus, "Der goldene Vogel," in *Grimms Märchen tiefenpsychologisch gedeutet* (Olten and Freiburg, 1982), 2:39-40.

15. Plutarch's Osiris myth is reprinted in G. Roeder, *Urkunden zur Religion des Alten Ägyptens* (Jena, 1915), 15-21 (chap. 14, p. 17).

On the figure of Anubis see W. Helck, "Ägypten: Die Mythologie der Ägypter," in H. W. Haussig, ed., *Wörterbuch der Mythologie*, vol. 1: *Götter und Mythen im Vorderen Orient* (Stuttgart, 1965), 334–36.

16. On the journeys of shamans to the Beyond see H. Findeisen and H. Gehrts, *Die Schamanen: Jagdhelfer und Ratgeber, Seelenfahrer, Künder, Heiler* (Cologne, 1983), 112–25 (on the shaman tree and ascent to heaven) and 226–44 (the story of the son of earth and his wife, the daughter of heaven). In Grimm's fairy tales the closest thing to this schema is the tale of "The Crystal Ball" (KHM 197). See Eugen Drewermann and Ingritt Neuhaus, "Die Kristallkugel," in *Grimms Märchen tiefenpsychologisch gedeutet* (Olten and Freiburg, 1985), vol. 6.

17. Thus, for example, the bear in the tale of "Snow White and Rose Red" (KHM 16). See Eugen Drewermann and Ingritt Neuhaus, "Schneeweisschen und Rosenrot," in *Grimms Märchen tiefenpsychologisch gedeutet* (Olten and Freiburg, 1983), 6:30–35.

18. CIT, no. 125, 780; see no. 126, 782–83.

19. CIT, no. 138, 803.

20. CIT, no. 135, 796.

21. TLP, 75.

22. WSS, chap. 8, "Prisoner of the Sand," 108–57.

23. See the Grimms' fairy tale "The Water of Life" (KHM 97), whose content and structure are in many ways similar to "The Golden Bird." See ibid., 52. In the New Testament the story of the woman at Jacob's well (Jn. 4:1–42) can serve as a comparison on this point, as can, to some extent, the account of the lame man at the well of Bethsaida (Jn. 5:1–9). In the Old Testament see Ex. 47:9.

Chapter 4
Of Love and Death, or the Window on the Stars

1. TLP, 71.

2. See Eugen Drewermann, "Vom Problem des Selbstmords oder von einer letzten Gnade der Natur," in *Psychoanalyse und Moraltheologie*, vol. 3, *An der Grenze des Lebens* (Mainz, 1984).

3. This is the explanation given by Buddha (Udhana VIII 8) in the rich palace of the woman Visakha Migaramata, whose granddaughter has died:

> Whatever suffering, pain, and mourning
> May be in this world, in their numberless forms,

> Come only because we hold things dear.
> If you hold nothing dear, pain comes not near you.
> Hence they are joyful ones, the ones released by pain,
> To whom nothing on earth is dear.
> If you desire the pure painless state,
> Then see to it that you hold nothing dear in the world.

Translation by H. Oldenberg, quoted in H. von Glasenapp, "Die Literaturen Indiens," in *Handbuch der Literaturwissenschaft*, ed. O. Walzel (Wildpark and Potsdam, 1929), 132.

4. See Eugene Drewermann, "Von der Geborgenheit im Ring der Zeit," in *Strukturen des Bösen* (3d expanded ed., 1981), 1:373–89.

5. On the structure and philosophy of the Mayan calendar see J. E. S. Thompson, *The Rise and Fall of Maya Civilization*, 256–69; W. Cordan, *Popol Vuh: Mythos und Geschichte der Maya* (Düsseldorf and Cologne, 1962), 182–89.

6. WSS, 202.

7. Esp. Albert Camus, *The Myth of Sisyphus*, trans. Justin O'Brien (New York: Random House, 1955), 15–16.

8. Thus, above all, Gabriel Marcel, *Homo Viator: Introduction to a Metaphysic of Hope*, trans. Emma Craufurd (Chicago: Henry Regnery, 1951), 70–71, where Marcel points to the "indissoluble connection of love and hope."

9. W. Lennig, *Edgar Allan Poe in Selbstzeugnissen und Bilddokumenten* (Hamburg, 1959), 138–39, 148–50.

10. *Major Writers of America*, shorter ed., ed. Perry Miller et al. (New York: Harcourt, Brace & World, 1966), 119.

11. A. Gardiner, *Egyptian Grammar*, 3d ed. (Oxford, 1957), 568; *mnj* = land, written with the determinative of a man or mummy lying on the ground, has the meaning of death.

12. Ibid., 563, 576.

13. Joseph von Eichendorff, *Ausgewählte Werke*, ed. P. Stapf, vol. 1: *Gedichte und Romanze*, vol. 2: *Ahnung und Gegenwart* (Wiesbaden [Tempel Klassiker] n.d.), 1:265: "Spruch."

14. In a poem "To Julie" Novalis (*Werke*, edited and commented on by G. Schulz, 2d. rev. ed. [Munich, 1981], 84–85) could write:

> That I with nameless joy
> Am your companion in life
> And feed, profoundly moved,
> On the miracle of your creation —
> That we are betrothed in our innermost heart,

And I am yours, and you mine,
And this one chose me,
We have the sweet creature to thank
That lovingly chose us.
Oh, let us faithfully revere him,
Then we remain embodied as one.
If his love forever drives us on,
Nothing will disturb our alliance.
At his side we can confidently
Bear the burden of life
And blissfully tell one another:
His kingdom of heaven begins right now,
We shall, when we disappear from here,
Find one another in his arm.

On Novalis's relationship with the thirteen-year-old Sophie von Kühn see O. Betz, *Novalis: In Einverständnis mit dem Geheimnis,* Herder paperback 773 (1980), 13.

15. On Saint-Exupéry's close kinship with Nietzsche see Luc Estang, *Saint-Exupéry,* 25–26. The similarity of Nietzsche's boyhood to the psychic circumstances of Saint-Exupéry's early childhood, as we have reconstructed it here, is discussed in L. Frenzel's *Friedrich Nietzsche in Selbstzeugnissen und Bilddokumenten* (Hamburg: rororo, 1966), 8–16. There too we find the same overemphasis on being spoiled by the women who raised them, the same loneliness, the (homosexually tinged) differentness, the later transfiguration of the parent's house, the "masculine protest" as a life line.

16. Thus, for instance, in the Grimms' fairy tale, "The Water of Life" (KHM 97) or "The Blue Light" (KHM 116). It seems to be an ineradicable prejudice of Jung's disciples that narratives such as fairy tales must at all cost be read "integratively." Obviously *The Little Prince* ends with the separation of the child from the flyer, and Luc Estang rightly says, "The Little Prince remained on the sand, and he melted into it to create a new personage, the Great Caïd, builder of the Citadel" (*Saint-Exupéry,* 29). In contrast, A. Heimler manages to read the return of the Little Prince as "the highpoint of ego-integration," as a "way of coping with anxiety and finding the thou... in the face of death" ("Der kleine Prinz," in *Selbsterfahrung und Glaube,* 246).

17. For the way depth psychology interprets this structure see Eugen Drewermann, *Tiefenpsychologie und Exegese,* vol. 1, *Die Wahrheit der Formen: Von Traum, Mythos, Sage und Legende* (Olten and Freiburg, 1984), 198.

18. Anthony Quinn describes the great failed actor pleading, "Kid, help me . . . , help me, or we'll both drown" (*The Original Sin* [Boston: Little, Brown, 1972], 310-11). The "kid" disappears when the actor discovers love. The departure of the "kid" here is identical to the actor's integration. Meanwhile the Little Prince comes like an alien, a very lovable, but basically intrusive visitor, to the flyer. He makes no contribution whatsoever to repairing the motor. His departure is a genuine splitting off, a mixture of libido regression and dissociation in the ego.

PART TWO: QUESTIONS AND ANALYSES
Chapter 5
The Mystery of the Rose

1. TLP, 8.
2. On the concept and interpretation of "screen memories," see Eugen Drewermann, *Tiefenpsychologie und Exegese*, 1:350-68.
3. On the symbolic unity of the snake and the woman, see F. Neumann, *The Great Mother: An Analysis of the Archetype*, trans. Ralph Mannheim (New York: Pantheon, 1954), 187; see Eugen Drewermann, *Strukturen des Bösen*, 2:69-87, on the unity of earth, moon, snake, woman, and fertility. A. Heimler quite correctly sees in the snake symbolism a "child's nightmare" ("Der kleine Prinz," in *Selbsterfahrung und Glaube*, 200). But he immediately wastes this insight by quite arbitrarily associating with it a child who is "left all alone" and "cries in the night for its mother." Actually, it's just the opposite. Heimler's interpretation is still further off the mark when after abstractly diagnosing the boa as a certain "being-in-the-world" he then sees it in arbitrarily concrete fashion as an "arms race" or "economic competition."
4. Thus, for example, in the fairy tale "The Two Brothers" (KHM 60) or, transformed, in "The Crystal Ball" (KHM 197). See Eugen Drewermann and Ingritt Neuhaus, "Die Kristallkugel," *Grimms Märchen tiefenpsychologisch gedeutet* (Olten and Freiburg, 1985), vol. 6.
5. TLP, 26. Like most of Saint-Exupéry's biographers (see chap. 6 n. 3 below) Maria de Crisenoy thinks the rose is connected with certain of her subject's memories from the first period of his engagement.

"Saint-Exupéry, who found unforgettable words for friendship, will never speak of love again. And yet! Fifteen years later the Little Prince will be in love with a rose, a coquettish, difficult flower" (*Antoine de Saint-Exupéry: Poète et aviateur* [Paris: Spes, 1948], 64, 70, 175). The relationship between Bernis and Geneviève in *South Mail* undoubtedly *is* patterned on the experiences of Saint-Exupéry's failed first love. But in interpreting *The Little Prince*, this particular revelation of "Saint-Exupéry's psychic life" (Crisenoy, ibid., 180) we can't be satisfied with a reading that above all fails to explain the return of the Little Prince (the child Saint-Exupéry) to the rose.

6. TLP, 27.

7. TLP, 11.

8. The spherical form of the planet can be interpreted psychologically as a symbol of the female breast. Only by keeping this in mind can we understand how the Little Prince never suffers from hunger or thirst on his planet. To the astonishment of the flyer he continues to possess this capacity on earth as well. This compels us to suspect that behind this freedom from need must lie an extremely spoiled orality, an idea that is further underlined by the Little Prince's tiny stature and the relatively large size of his planet. Above all we can't grasp the reason for the deserted loneliness of the Little Prince on his planet unless we see in the entire planet an (oral) symbol of the mother who is and means the whole world to the child, without, however, being discovered in the process as a particular "person."

9. The sweeping of the volcanoes is an expressly anal activity. Here the potential eruptions of the craters could be interpreted not just as "uncleanliness" (going in one's pants), but they could also symbolize aggressive stirrings of the first phase of defiance. These oral-depressive features are now joined by strong compulsive features – the picture of a personality that can be attested to in every line Saint-Exupéry wrote, especially *Citadelle*. R. Zeller sees "love" and "hope" in the volcanoes, but of course there is no basis for such statements (*La vie secrète d'Antoine de Saint-Exupéry ou la parabole du petit prince* [Paris, 1950], 93ff).

10. In his "life chronicle" of Saint-Exupéry Luc Estang mentions that in 1904 his mother left the house in Lyon with her three daughters and two sons (151). Thereafter Antoine spent his childhood in two castles, which belonged to an aunt of his mother and to his maternal grandmother. See Pierre Chevrier, *Saint-Exupéry* (Paris: Gallimard, 1958), 17. None of his biographers considers it worthwhile to discuss what psychic conflicts may have arisen for Saint-Exupéry because of these moves. In *La vie secrète d'Antoine de Saint-Exupéry*, 31, R. Zeller does

speak of Saint-Exupéry's "loneliness" ("the loneliness was inside him," 34) and explains, "He was always lonely" (25). Ultimately the whole world echoes in the Little Prince's "I am all alone" (TLP, 61). But, like all the other biographers, Zeller thinks about the loneliness in a purely phenomenological, not a psychological, manner. In this way the causes are confused with the effects: Saint-Exupéry's loneliness is glorified as a "longing for infinity" (Zeller, ibid., 34). Zeller even speaks of "the flyer's trust in his spiritual loneliness" (31). But even when biographical and psychological connections are made between the Little Prince and the rose, some interpreters of the rose (e.g., Luc Estang, *Saint-Exupéry,* 33–34) conjecture that this is simply Saint-Exupéry's recollections of the broken engagement with his first fiancée. Yet even Estang recognizes that the planet of the rose is to be understood as Saint-Exupéry's childhood, not his engagement (35).

Furthermore the Little Prince's return fits only one woman in Saint-Exupéry's life, his mother. Finally, even (and especially) in first adolescent love, memories of one's own mother revive with vehement force. The grounds for the failure of Saint-Exupéry's first love might well be sought in the same ambivalent feelings that characterized the bonding with his mother. See chap. 6 n. 3 below. On the chronology of Saint-Exupéry's life, see P. Kessel, *La vie de Saint-Exupéry* (Paris, 1954), 6–27 (childhood and youth).

11. TLP, 20. In "Der kleine Prinz," in *Selbsterfahrung und Glaube,* 211, A. Heimler very pointedly suggests that behind the Prince's anxiety over the "rose" we can recognize "forbidden aggressive feelings toward the flower." "The fear of oral (verbal) aggression" really exists, but here too Heimler fails to make use of his own finding. He turns a conflicted relationship between the Prince and the "rose" into a conflict between "consciousness" and the "unconscious," even though he also considers the possibility that it refers to the "encounter with a real woman" (241).

12. TLP, 28. A. Heimler makes the excellent suggestion that the sheep is another form of the boa, which "[has been] transformed under continual pressure from the self into a little lamb" ("Der kleine Prinz," in *Selbsterfahrung und Glaube,* 204–5). But apart from the fact that nobody is likely to have any idea what "continual pressure from the self" is supposed to mean, this puzzling typological-symbolic interpretation creates more difficulties than it solves. The real problem of the sheep is the muzzle and the threat to the rose; hence this must be the point of departure for any interpretation.

13. TLP, 12.

14. TLP, 28.

15. Ibid.

16. "Nefertem" actually means "the wholly perfect one," the "fully beautiful one," and is "the lotus flower on the nose of Ra," as the Pyramid texts say (H. Kees, *Der Götterglaube im Alten Ägypten,* 89). In the New Kingdom the canonical trinity was thought to be Ptah, Sechmet, and Nefertem (Kees, ibid., 287).

17. Luc Estang remarks about the writer's relationship with his wife, "He actually paraphrases, with minor deviations, the famous maxim [of Nietzsche] that 'the man should be trained for war, and woman for the recreation of the warrior' " (*Saint-Exupéry par lui-même,* 37). "His biographers recount that Saint-Exupéry himself applied this principle to the 'nice beetles,' as he called them." In *Citadelle* Saint-Exupéry goes so far as to reduce love itself to a mere symbol: "Perhaps the truth is that the love of the wife who awaits the return of her husband is not so important. The hand that waves before his departure is not so important. But it is a sign of something important." " . . . Thus geometry is a symbol, but so are those arms that a husband throws around his wife, who is pregnant, heavy with a world within her, and whom he protects" (no. 21, 580). For someone like Saint-Exupéry a woman's love is especially dangerous as a temptation to "rest." "Likewise, one doesn't rest in love, if it does not transform itself from day to day, as in motherhood. But you want to sit in your gondola and to become the gondolier's song for life. And you're wrong. For all whatever is neither ascent nor passage is meaningless. And if you stop on the way, you will find nothing but boredom, because the landscape has nothing more to teach you. And you will reject the woman, when it's you that should have been rejected to begin with" (CIT, no. 35, 611). Nietzsche would have said the exact same thing.

The fantasies of the ruler in CIT revolve with striking frequency around "dancing girls, singing girls, and courtesans" (see no. 37, 614). The "Caid" expressly warns about the "woman . . . who adores herself," who "devours, without nourishing herself," who "is out for booty in love" (no. 170, 864-65) — woman as potential vampire. This is the anxiety-ridden side of Saint-Exupéry's attitude toward woman as the snake. Love as obligation is the formula for this feeling, only under the semblance of a moral postulate.

E. A. Racky objectively has the right explanation, but without noticing the psychological problem here: "Saint-Exupéry can't even see his way to the modern version of companionship between a man and woman, nor do we hear a word about love with a capital L." "Saint-Exupéry meets woman with a distinctly chivalrous politeness, with reverence. Women are fragile and tender. They mustn't be touched with rough hands. Woman doesn't have the possibility of taking part in action or of experiencing the all-sacrificing friendship of the male community. . . . When he's among the flyers, Saint-Exupéry thinks he can overcome the difficulties of understanding the other. Male friendship forges bonds that reveal one friend's inner life to the other. But woman continues to be a mystery" (*Die Auffassung vom Menschen bei Antoine de Saint-Exupéry*, 34–35). One couldn't find a better description of Saint-Exupéry's latent homosexuality and flight from women.

Speaking of one of his dancing girls, whom in his boredom he finally chooses to be his bride, the ruler in CIT declares: "You are nothing but a step on my ascent to God. . . . You are made to be burned, consumed, but not to be held" (no. 29, 599). R. Zeller admittedly recognizes the difference between such viewpoints and the position, for instance, of Christianity, but in this same passage he maintains that "Saint-Exupéry [managed to reconcile] . . . his longing for space with the love of woman" (*L'homme et le navire de Saint-Exupéry*, 89). But what are we to make of a "reconciliation" that burns the woman as a witch, so as to lift one's own soul to heaven in the ecstasy of her annihilation?

There are passages where the reader has to understand Saint-Exupéry rather than believe him. Daniel Anet has a point when he argues that "the true role Saint-Exupéry gave woman" was "the young girl" (*Antoine de Saint-Exupéry: Poète-Romancier-Moraliste* [Paris: Corrêa, 1946], 207). But instead of seeing in this a psychological problem – fear of grown women, the psychic block of a frightened child – Anet goes so far as to declare, in all seriousness, that while the young girls may not "swallow up the destiny of the men, they justify it in their brilliant purity, in their silent love" (212). Anet then proceeds to talk about the "heroes" among the men.

18. TLP, 31.

19. TLP, 30.

20. TLP, 31.

21. The "drafts" and the "cough" surely have to be read as a psychic "cold." On the psychosomatic disturbances of respiration see Martha W. Gerard, "Bronchial Asthma in Children," 245–48, in Franz Alexander, *Studies in Psychosomatic Medicine* (New York: Ronald Press, 1948), 99–104. Gerard particularly addresses the psychic dependency, the separation trauma in colds affecting the respiratory tract. The decidedly aggressive meaning of a cough is practically proverbial.

22. TLP, 32.

23. Ibid.

24. Ibid. "Rose, oh pure contradiction, what pleasure / To be no one's sleep under so many / Eyelids" is the epitaph that Rainer Maria Rilke chose for himself. "In his lifetime the rose, that ancient western symbol for the unio mystica, was for Rilke a source of ecstasy and brooding devotion" (H. E. Holthusen, *Rainer Maria Rilke in Selbstzeugnissen und Bilddokumenten* [Hamburg: rororo, 1964], 163). This is the epitaph of a man who "while loving, cannot love" (ibid., 132), because his relationship with his fellow men and women was continually and unhappily thwarted by the contradictory bond to his mother (ibid., 11–20). At age twenty-one Rilke had met Lou Andreas Salomé (fifteen years his senior), who gave him his first complete experience of love, the happiness "of being understood and led by a kindred and yet superior spirit, and of being allowed at the same time to discover in his beloved the mother figure he was so painfully deprived of" (ibid., 33). The friendship between Rilke and Lou Salomé was lifelong. Saint-Exupéry, by contrast, was never granted such happiness. In addition he fought off, although not very successfully, the softening influence of his mother, and hence of every other woman. This, of course, cost him a great deal of inner division, as we have seen.

25. TLP, 34.

26. Ibid.

27. Ibid. A. Heimler rightly notes that the Little Prince is surprised when the rose takes responsibility this time ("Der kleine Prinz," in *Selbsterfahrung und Glaube,* 216). But he gets things backward when he reads this statement by the rose as a "free-spirited declaration of love," which makes the Little Prince afraid to come near her. Instead it causes guilt feelings before his departure, which is the danger in the rose's behavior.

28. TLP, 34.

29. TLP, 93.

30. *Lettres à sa mère* (Paris: Gallimard, 1955), 70.

31. Ibid., 74.

32. Ibid., 93–94.

33. Ibid., 94.

34. Ibid.

35. Ibid., 126.

36. Ibid., 130–31.

37. Ibid., 147.

38. Ibid., 161.

39. Ibid., 154–55.

40. Ibid., 170.

Chapter 6
The Mystery of Icarus

1. This point is made in particular by R. M. Albérès: "In Saint-Exupéry the poetry of flight is not merely observation of nature, but contact with the forces of nature" (*Saint-Exupéry* [Paris, 1946], 83). René Delange makes a case like Albérès's in René Delange and Léon Werth, *La vie de Saint-Exupéry, suivi de "Tel que je l'ai connu"* (Paris: Éditions du Seuil, 1948), 11–26. See also C. Cate, *Antoine de Saint-Exupéry*, 143–58. L. Wencelius even recognizes "in the heroic life of the air-explorers the knights of the old sagas, fighting with the dragons of the South Atlantic" ("Saint-Exupéry der Freund," in *Romania* [Mainz, 1948], 1:47–62, 52). This sort of estimation of Saint-Exupéry follows to the letter the myth that he himself created – obviously with complete success – about himself. W. Kellermann presents a similar view in "Antoine de Saint-Exupéry," in *Die Sammlung* 2 (1947), Göttingen, 679–94. On 683 he writes: "The flyer exchanges his ethos of struggle for every renunciation of safety and happiness. But in return he gains the noble absorption in the cosmic loneliness of the night, whose greatness the poet...characterizes with the language of the fairy tale, legend, and religion." As if the technique of flying didn't consist precisely in putting a stop to adventures and eliminating every accident through careful planning. That is, or at least ought to be, the technician's "responsibility."

2. On the figure of Eros see Robert Graves, *The Greek Myths*, 2 vols. (Harmondsworth: Penguin, 1980), 1:58–59. On the interpretation of eros as the principle of longing for immortality see Plato, *The Symposium* 207a 5–208 b6.

3. See chap. 5 n. 10 and n. 17 above. C. Cate, for example, does take pains to describe Saint-Exupéry's marriage (1931) with Consuelo Suncin, the widow of the Argentine journalist Gomez Carrillo, in the most romantic terms (*Antoine de Saint-Exupéry*, 171–82). But even in Cate's presentation we can sense that the bride must have been feeling the fascination of love far more than the groom. In later years it turned out that Consuelo had a hard time putting up with Saint-Exupéry's stern, inexorable nature, and sought relief "in her...wild fantasy" (Cate, 404) and in her friendships with a chosen circle of famous surrealists in her New York exile. We may wonder how long their relationship would have lasted had it not been for Saint-Exupéry's early death. How long could it have survived if Saint-Exupéry hadn't been able to spend his life on continual vacations from family life, thanks to his flying? K. Rauch cites a

prayer that Saint-Exupéry had his wife Consuelo say, and he sees in it the manifestation of a straightforward and pure trust in God, together with the intimate and equally pure love between man and wife" ("Antoine de Saint-Exupéry: Mensch und Werk," 25, 26). But the prayer is basically a request to Consuelo "not to see any of those people whom he despises and rejects," as well as a confession that "he may seem to look strong, but he's always all too fearful..." "Lord, please, above all spare him the fear!" On Saint-Exupéry's image of God and his relationship to prayer, see chap. 6 n. 37 and n. 38 below.

On the way Saint-Exupéry presents, in *South Mail,* the (unhappy) affair between Bernis and Geneviève, evidently working into it his own recollections of the love for his fiancée at the time, Louise de Vilmorin (1922), see Luc Estang, *Saint-Exupéry,* 34-37; 48-49; 67; C. Cate, *Saint-Exupéry,* 63-68. Cate rightly argues that the Little Prince's rose can scarcely be identical to Louise, noting that Louise was two years younger than Saint-Exupéry and had not "yet been ripe for marriage" (74). This is exactly the reverse reason why the relationship of the Little Prince with the rose comes to grief. K. Rauch tries to clear up the question of why the world of women plays no role in *The Little Prince:* "The Little Prince has a child's soul and it stands over against the stiff grown-up world of all the various masculine and ego-entrapped rulers of the planets he visits, all of whom he perceives as very strange and alien. On the other hand he feels a supple familiarity with the organic wisdom of the unselfconscious creatures, the animal world, and the fox. For him everything emotionally feminine is concentrated in the rose, whom he loves so shyly and tenderly, whom he reveres so sensuously. In the end he flees back, after planet earth makes him feel the lack of all warmth and intimacy" ("Antoine de Saint-Exupéry: Mensch und Werk," 25). This is correct and well said, but it masks the condition in Saint-Exupéry that set him at loggerheads with the world around him: his central ambivalence toward the bond with his mother. Rauch obscures the real point in Saint-Exupéry's "longing for the maternal." It's no use glorifying Saint-Exupéry; we have to understand him if we are to grasp his greatness as well as his limits.

4. On the biographical connection of flying with the Icarus motif, see Luc Estang, *Saint-Exupéry:* "By this time [i.e., 1926] a Saint-Exupéryan sadness has already appeared in his letters. The mystique of the airline saved him from it and transforms it into compassion. But as soon as the lovely adventure of flying is over, anxiety puts on its old mask" (45-48, 183).

5. The image of Saint-Exupéry as a great friend and comrade like-

wise follows the quite deliberately framed myth. In fact even C. Cate
has to admit that the "age difference" with his comrades made personal
relations difficult, and despite "all his efforts [Saint-Ex felt like]...an
outsider" (*Saint-Exupéry*, 394). On the doctrine of "comradeship" and
"fellowship of the deed," see Luc Estang, *Saint-Exupéry*, 73–81. The
quintessence of this attitude is: "Life has taught us that love does not
consist in gazing at each other, but looking outward together in the same
direction" (WSS, 195). Obviously Saint-Exupéry is mistaking comradeship for love, or explaining that he can barely imagine any other kind
of love except the quest for comrades. The problem is always the same.
You can't love people if they (and you!) can be created as human beings
only through the heroism of the deed. In FTA Saint-Exupéry explains:
"The notion of looking on at life has always been hateful to me. What am
I if not a participant? In order to be, I must participate. I am fed by the
quality that resides in those who participate with me....The presence
of these men is dense, full of meaning, and it warms my heart" (398).

That's how Saint-Exupéry wanted things. But was it really that way?
E. A. Racky argues: "The active person's sense of being bonded to everyone else is deepened in the group of fliers through the friendship and
comradeship that Saint-Exupéry experienced in such a pure form that
he looked on them as essential values for all people" (*Die Auffassung
vom Menschen bei Antoine de Saint-Exupéry*, 28). But in fact Racky is
confusing the idea with reality. Luc Estang shows how in reality his
"comrades" could take cruel revenge on the author of *Night Flight*
(*Saint-Exupéry*, 180).

Indeed, even if Saint-Exupéry had found among his comrades the
warmth he needed, he would have been incapable of accepting it. His
longing is actually directed to the unreachable. "To be more than myself.
To possess this plenitude that swells so powerfully within me. To feel
the love that I feel for the Group, a love that is not an impulse from
without but is something inward and never to be manifested – except
at a farewell dinner....My love of the Group has no need of definition. It
is woven of bonds" (FTA, 400). One could hardly give clearer expression
to fear of a real (homosexual) bond and to its replacement by the pride
of renunciation.

6. *Kriegesbriefe an einen Freund* (War Letters to a Friend), in
Gesammelte Schriften in 3 Bänden (Munich: DTV, 1978), 3:175–76.
A. Heimler correctly recognizes in the motif of flying a "breaking away
from Mother Earth through one's own power" ("Der kleine Prinz," in
Selbsterfahrung und Glaube, 206). But since he always reads *The Little
Prince* archetypally instead of – to start with, anyway – biographi-

cally, Heimler misses the obvious: Saint-Exupéry's flight from his own mother. Instead of this Heimler claims this is the antithesis between the "heavenly" (yang) and the "earthly" (yin).

7. See Karl Stern, *The Flight from Woman* (New York: Noonday, 1965), who lays special stress on the Manichaean feature of modernity.

8. On Saint-Exupéry's affinity to Nietzsche see Luc Estang, *Saint-Exupéry*, 37–38, 113. For Saint-Exupéry, as for Nietzsche, "The individuals are only ways and transitions" (FTA, 417). The goal of this "way" is the heroic individual, who is always healthy and strong. The heroic notion always sees the possible hero in a person...L'homme d'action reveals... clear features of the superman" (E. A. Racky, *Die Auffassung vom Menschen bei Antoine de Saint-Exupéry*, 80). Saint-Exupéry himself says: "I shall fight against all those who, maintaining that my charity pays homage to mediocrity, would destroy Man and thus imprison the individual in an irredeemable mediocrity. I shall fight for Man. Against Man's enemies – but against myself as well" (FTA, 435). There is no recognizable difference between the viewpoint of such passages and Nietzsche's "love of the farthest away" (as opposed to love of one's neighbor), with all its contempt for real people.

9. On J.-P. Sartre's philosophy of freedom in the realm of radical contingency see Eugen Drewermann, *Strukturen des Bösen*, 3:207–9, 213–18, 226–63. Karl Stern analyzes the revulsion from nature (and himself) in Sartre as fear of woman, arguing: "The way the sexual invariably has the connotation of a visit-to-a-certain-house, together with the devaluation of the womanly, reminds one of the pubescent Manichaeism which pervades so much of the nineteenth century, all the way from Nietzsche to Lenin. It is interesting in this context that the only scene in the entire work of Sartre which suggests love is the death of a man in the arms of his comrade (in 'Drôle d'Amitié')" (*The Flight from Woman*, 138).

The whole psychological structure of thinking: the activist striving to overcome the shameful nothingness of the ego, the fear of woman (the mother), the (latently homosexual) equating of love and death, and beyond that the stifling mixture of excessive psychic strain and coddling with material things – all this can be demonstrated, for all their temperamental and individual differences, in the work of Nietzsche, Sartre, and Saint-Exupéry. On the childhood of Sartre, who like Saint-Exupéry, grew up without a father in a "strange" family, see W. Biemel, *Jean-Paul Sartre in Selbstzeugnissen und Bilddokumenten* (Hamburg: rororo, 1964), 7–24. Biemel lays particular stress on "pretending, always being good, having to orient oneself toward others" (20–21).

154 ᑯ Notes to Page 106

10. On the mixture of arrogance and modesty in Sartre see W. Biemel, *Jean-Paul Sartre*, 93–102.

11. In fact for Saint-Exupéry "flying" means no more or less than the justification for being in this world. See Luc Estang, *Saint-Exupéry*, 179–80. Estang underlines Saint-Exupéry's depressive game with death, which from 1931 on (when he left the airmail service) was his primary response to life, and which led to certain suicidal reactions as early as 1933, when he had the accident in the bay of Saint-Raphael.

12. P. Federn points especially to the phallic significance of "flying," which can be described, in terms of subjective experience, by the emotional qualities of masculine greatness, intoxicating achievement, and mystical union, in other words by the things that Saint-Exupéry found so fascinating in flight ("Über zwei typische Traumsensationen," in Sigmund Freud, ed., *Jahrbuch der Psychoanalyse*, 6:128). R. Delange cites the address given by Lieutenant Gelée on the occasion of Saint-Exupéry's death: "Anyone who knew him only from a distance can see all sorts of things in him: a poet and moralist, an intellectual, even a magician. But we, his brothers, know better. We know that he was above all a flyer, a pilot, a creature of the air. Not for empty fame, not for carefully thought up and thoroughly exploited social considerations, but because he had a vocation, a passion for it. Will literary critics ever grasp that?" (*La vie d'Antoine de Saint-Exupéry*, 130). They will grasp it, not by lending credence to the myth of Saint-Exupéry the flyer, but by trying to understand the man who took refuge in his airplane to escape the earth. Lieutenant Gelée continues: "Saint-Exupéry was indebted to practically no one. He owed his uniqueness only to his life and his craft whose heroic age he was part of" (130).

That's just what Saint-Exupéry wanted to be: giving to others without receiving, seeking his own greatness in the struggle against himself and the mediocrity of the average existence. K. Rauch explains: "For him [Saint-Exupéry] flying meant moving on to a fresh discovery of the world. In his sensibility climbing into the air – the fulfillment of that primeval dream of humankind that Greek and German legends had long ago been concerned with – corresponded to an enhancement of all humanity's inborn possibilities" ("Antoine de Saint-Exupéry: Weg und Werk," 2:155). See Rauch's "Antoine de Saint-Exupéry: Mensch und Werk," where flying is described as the "union of organism and machine," as an unswerving charge forward, as the conquering of completely new existential space" (53). This assessment naturally includes Saint-Exupéry's poetic greatness in describing flight, which Jules Roy rightly compares with Joseph Conrad's description of the sea and sailing (*Passion de Saint-Exupéry* [Paris, 1951], 27–36).

13. Laurette Séjourné sees in the "feathered serpent" an image of the rising sun, the sky, spirit (= a bird), matter, as well as the female divinities of the earth, nothingness, and death (= the snake) (*Altamerikanische Kulturen* [Frankfurt: Fischer, 1971], 276).

14. Thus, for example, in the Grimms' fairy tale of the crystal ball (KHM 197), where two sons of a sorceress are transformed into an eagle and a whale. See Eugen Drewermann and Ingritt Neuhaus, "Die Kristall-kugel," in *Grimms Märchen tiefenpsychologisch gedeutet* (Olten and Freiburg, 1985), vol. 6.

15. FTA, 307.

16. *Kriegesbriefe an einen Freund* (War Letters to a Friend), 3: 176–77.

17. E. A. Racky gives an incisive sketch of *l'homme de l'action,* the man of action, who is shaped by the varieties of resistance he meets, which force him to grow beyond himself (*Die Auffassung vom Menschen bei Antoine de Saint-Exupéry,* 26–38). He also feels bonded to others as their comrade through his activity or through the obligation that his activity places him under: "Happiness is not the goal of his striving, but a gift...like beauty" (ibid., 31).

18. CIT, no. 112, 755, or CIT, no. 190, 903.

19. TLP, 73–74

20. CIT, no. 56, 649.

21. Most of Saint-Exupéry's biographers characterize his childhood as thoroughly happy, but without describing it. For example, René De-lange has nothing to say about his childhood before age ten, except for the fact that he was experimenting with verse as early as six years of age ("Antoine de Saint-Exupéry," in René Delange and Léon Werth, *La vie de Saint-Exupéry,* 7). The same treatment occurs in K. Rauch. Rauch relies on information from Saint-Exupéry's sister Simone and, above all, on the close relationship of Antoine with his nursemaid Paula Hentschel ("Antoine de Saint-Exupéry: Mensch und Werk," 23). But none of the biographers considers it necessary to discuss honestly the psychic background of Saint-Exupéry's early childhood development.

Maria de Crisenoy picks up the story of how Antoine (see FTA, 316–18) played sick in hopes of getting attention from the "sisters in the white cornets," only to feel all the more excluded by his classmates (*Antoine de Saint-Exupéry,* 13–14). But Crisenoy too fails to reflect on the bind that is so characteristic of Saint-Exupéry's whole life: longing for love that he doesn't find in weakness and doesn't need in strength.

The ambivalences and blind alleys of these childhood impressions have not, so far as I can see, been seriously analyzed by any of Saint-Exupéry's biographers. Instead the reader is forever being told, as in H. G. Nauen, "Antoine de Saint-Exupéry: Leben und Werk" (*Stimmen der Zeit* 153 [1953–54], 154–66): "Saint-Exupéry must have had a dreamily beautiful youth, a real paradise of innocence and bliss. From it continually flowed invisible sources of strength that never quite let him despair even in the bitterest moments of his life. He himself is the Little Prince who fell to this planet like a star from the sky" (105).

Even Luc Estang, who on the whole maintains some critical distance from his work, considers Saint-Exupéry the "happiest of children... [a happiness that came] not only from living in a noble mansion, from romping about in old parks, from listening in enchantment to the Tyrolian governess Paula, and from holding sway over the most maternal of mothers and the most devoted brothers and sisters" (*Saint-Exupéry*, 26–35). It's true, Saint-Exupéry kept yearning for these childhood days, so they must have had some bright sides. But evidently none of the biographers are willing or able to realize that this sort of "beautiful childhood" can be a pitfall, as it had the power to poison all the rest of his life with fear and melancholy, and at the same time led to that desperate battle against being stifled by his mother that would later transform the Little Prince into "le grand Caïd."

J.-C. Ibert correctly sees the lay of the land, though without any psychological insight, when he writes: "Beyond action and mysticism there is in Saint-Exupéry the myth of innocence and rediscovered childhood." Saint-Exupéry felt "exiled from his childhood, and in his work he often nostalgically conjures up these years untouched by care" (*Antoine de Saint-Exupéry, suivi de la "Lettre au Général X"* [Paris: Éditions Universitaires, 1953], 79). Conversely he sees in the Little Prince a double of Saint-Exupéry himself. But as a matter of course this lays the blame for the contradictions in Saint-Exupéry, i.e., in the man himself, at the door of the "wicked world," thereby defending Saint-Exupéry the child. There is a great danger here of reading into *The Little Prince* one's own childhood wishes, one's own unfulfilled dreams and disappointments with life, and so turning this wonderful fairy tale into a Bible for the frustrated. One really must understand the danger implied in "years untouched by care," i.e., the coddling of a fatherless childhood. Even as a forty-year-old man how energetically, but also how wearily Saint-Exupéry tried to fight off certain remnants of his childhood coddling, as he himself describes in FTA: "Yet this body had to be withdrawn from beneath the eiderdown; it had to be washed in freezing water, shaved, dressed, made respectable before presenting it-self to the bursts of steel. And getting out of bed was like a return to infancy, like being torn from the maternal arms, the maternal breast, from everything that cherishes, caresses, shelters the existence of the infant" (ibid., 330). Obviously the psychological difficulty here lies in understanding that a certain kind of overindulgence, spoiling, and pam-pering can make a child just as neurotic as can excessive strictness. In any event, the tensions that were built into Saint-Exupéry's devel-opment from the very beginning can never be understood if we take the usual approach of setting off the Little Prince against the uncom-prehending world of the "big persons." That externalizes the conflict in oneself, merely succumbing to the seduction of the charming "sun king" (which Saint-Exupéry admittedly was), to transcribing legends. Or else one condemns oneself to piling up unanswerable questions. In reality the "heroic concept of man" in Saint-Exupéry was designed to prove that he wasn't a mama's boy. He indicates this himself in WSS, where half a lifetime later he reproaches his housekeeper, Miss Sophie, telling her how wrong she was with all the exaggerated concern in her fears and warnings: "Do you know, there are deserts where one sleeps outdoors in the cold night, without a roof, auntie, without a bed and without sheets?" (ibid., 108). And yet at the same instant Saint-Exupéry longs to go back to his "beautiful" childhood, to his mother, to the nurse-maid Paula. See R. Zeller, *La vie secrète d'Antoine de Saint-Exupéry* (Paris, 1950), 39–40.

22. CIT, no. 49, 647–48.

23. CIT, no. 25, 590.

24. CIT, no. 126, 784. Saint-Exupéry explains with disarming open-ness, "The dignity of the individual demands that he not be reduced to vassalage by the largesse of others" (FTA, 430). And conversely: "I understand no men except those to whom I give" (FTA, 403). G. Pelissier does offer an explanation to justify Saint-Exupéry's attitude: "If I seek, I have found, because the mind longs only for what it already has. Find-ing is seeing. And how would I seek anything that didn't already have some feeling for me?" ("Introduction à la lecture de 'Citadelle,'" Oeu-vre posthume de Saint-Exupéry," in *Synthèses* 6 [1951], 306). But this is Pascal speaking (*Pensées,* Brunschvicg no. 555), not Saint-Exupéry; and it's true only if one is, like Pascal, referring to a person's absolute longing for God. It is utterly false to apply the same principle to the rela-tionship between a man and a woman. Furthermore Pascal was aiming to calm the metaphysical anxiety of the individual ("Be not disturbed"), while Saint-Exupéry is using his artificial theorem to justify his fear

of any kind of intimacy with women as well as his glorification of the sacrificial "quest."

25. TLP, 71.

26. TLP, 70. These are the same words used concerning "the young girls" in Saint-Exupéry's letters to Lucie-Marie Décour.

27. See Friedrich Schiller, "Über Anmut und Würde" (1793), in Schiller, *Werke,* ed. P. Stapf (Wiesbaden, n.d.), 2:505, 526.

28. For example, E. Racky writes concerning *Night Flight:* "Rivière wants the individual to grow beyond himself. These notions stem from Friedrich Nietzsche.... The chief demands of his flyers that they subordinate themselves completely to their common task. The work is everything and will survive the men. It gives them a share of eternity. Rivière calls for devotion, sacrifice, renunciation, and death for this work. He never asks whether his harsh demand destroys human happiness. For the chief, that is, for Saint-Exupéry, at the time when *Vol de nuit* appeared, the rule was: 'L'action brise le bonheur.' It's no surprise that certain critics saw in the young Saint-Exupéry a fascist" (*Die Auffassung vom Menschen bei Antoine de Saint-Exupéry,* 81–82). Racky tries to blunt this criticism by referring to the fact that for Saint-Exupéry there was "something enduring in Man." What then? — what if the individual bases himself purely on deeds, and if for Saint-Exupéry there is "happiness, fulfilment, and peace" only in death? (Racky, ibid., 86).

It's true that as early as *Wind, Sand, and Stars* Saint-Exupéry complemented his Nietzschean heroism with Christian-social attitudes of responsibility, which he also called "love." But he turns love into a cramped, voluntaristic sophistry when he explains "To create love, we must begin by sacrifice. Afterward, love will demand further sacrifices and ensure us every victory. But it is we who must take the first step. We must be born before we can exist" (FTA, 433).

29. CIT, no. 108, 745.

30. Nietzsche, *Thus Spoke Zarathustra,* trans. R. J. Hollingdale (Harmondsworth: Penguin, 1969), pt. 4, "The Sign," 336.

31. "He [Rivière] had reached a point where not the problem of a small personal grief but the very will to act was in itself an issue. Not so much Fabien's wife as another theory of life confronted Rivière now. Hearing that timid voice, he could but pity its infinite distress — and know it for an enemy! For action and individual happiness have no truck with each other; they are eternally at war. This woman, too, was championing a self-coherent world with its own rights and duties, that world where a lamp shines at nightfall, flesh calls to mated flesh, a homely world of love and hopes and memories. She stood up for happiness and

she was right. And Rivière, too, was right..." (NF, 260). " 'Under what authority [Rivière wonders] have I taken them from all this?' What was his right to rob them of their personal happiness? Did not the highest of all laws order that these human joys should be safeguarded?...And yet one day, inevitably, these golden sanctuaries vanish like a mirage. Old age and death, more pitiless than even he, destroy them. There is, perhaps, some other thing, something more lasting, to be saved; and, perhaps [!], it was to save this part of man that Rivière was working" (NF, 261). With all due respect for Saint-Exupéry, one has to say that this sort of philosophizing borders unintentionally on cynicism (NF, 262; see NF, 268–69).

Nevertheless there are critics who feel obliged to surpass Saint-Exupéry on this point as well. Thus G. Gehring argues: "No, Rivière is not heartless. He thinks pity is something good. But, unfortunately, the only thing that matters is the goal [!], and to reach it, one has to strike the evil where it appears. Above all one mustn't become weak!...The superior commands all the events, even should he be forced to crush people to pieces" ("Der heroische Humanismus bei Exupéry," in *Die lebenden Fremd-sprachen* 2 [1950], 5, 134). It is astonishing that something like this could be written only five years after the downfall of the Third Reich. But even critics like J.-C. Ibert agree with Rivière's philosophy: "The value of every step we take will be proportional to the effort we have to make to leave ourselves behind" (*Antoine de Saint-Exupéry*, 26). "What motive can be invoked to legitimize this refusal of earthly happiness? There is eternity, the conquest of the Absolute, victory over the fear of death....Indifferent to justice or injustice, Rivière gives a soul to human material" (28).

The result of this is "He himself [i.e., Fabien, who "sacrifices himself at Rivière's command] does not exist"! (29). "What is important is the way, not arriving at the goal" (ibid., 64). Rightly questioning this, H. G. Nauen asks: "Ultimately what can be said from the standpoint of Rivière's vague idea to condemn the shameful concentration camps of our time, where millions were sacrificed to a 'dubious goal'?" ("Antoine de Saint-Exupéry: Leben und Werk," 109). As early as 1932 Clifton Fadiman spoke of the "fascist terms" and the "febrile heroism" that in *Night Flight* Saint-Exupéry turns into virtues, arguing "that Saint-Exupéry's admittedly eloquent deifications of mere will and energy lead straight to Von Treitschke and the megalomania of Il Duce....This is...a dangerous book,...because it celebrates a pernicious idea by disguising it as a romantic emotion...because it lists a fine imaginative talent in the defense of a spiritual toryism" (quoted in Curtis Cate, *Antoine de*

Saint-Exupéry, 238–39, who tries in vain to shield Saint-Exupéry from this criticism).

Flight to Arras was also condemned, not altogether unfairly, by André Breton (a friend of the author's wife, Consuelo). Alexandre Koyré likewise found the book "fascistic" in its attitude, while its underlying philosophy was dismissed as "paternalistic" and reactionary" (Cate, 457). A. Fabri even said of *Citadelle*: "Just as Saint-Exupéry counterfeits distress as counsel, he passes off monologue as dialogue" ("Versuch über Exupérys 'Citadelle,' " in *Merkur* 5 [1951], 900). Above all Fabri is right to object to the "theatrically embarrassing melody" of "Je suis le chef. Je suis le maître. Je suis le responsable," which he calls "magisterial-apodictic."

Luc Estang's summary is fair: "The face of human creative will in Saint-Exupéry's work is too much like the face of the will to power, whether that of Rivière or the Caïd.... This hardness resembles that of the gardener who trims the tree and if necessary cuts down the neighboring trees. I see this perfectly well,... but human beings aren't trees" (Saint-Exupéry, 115). See WSS, where Saint-Exupéry compares the death of his comrade with the fall of great trees (26). Of course, R. Zeller is right too when he says that it is a "wonderful definition of man," to explain that "the tree is that power that slowly weds the sky" (*L'homme et le navire de Saint-Exupéry*, 83).

32. Eugen Drewermann, "Das Tragische und das Christliche," in *Psychoanalyse und Moraltheologie*, vol. 1, *Angst und Schuld* (Mainz, 1982), 39ff.

33. NF, 280.

34. W. Krickeberg, *Altmexikanische Kulturen*, 193–94. See also P. J. Schmidt, *Der Sonnenstein der Azteken* (Hamburg: Hamburgisches Museum für Völkerkunde, 1974), 9–12. The comparison with the ideas of Indian cultures is, by the way, something that occurred to Saint-Exupéry himself. He has Rivière think: "To love, only to love leads nowhere. Rivière knew a dark sense of duty, greater than that of love. And deep within it there might lie another emotion and a tender one, but worlds away from ordinary feelings. He recalled a phrase that he once had read: 'The one thing is to make them everlasting...' He remembered a temple of the sun-god, built by the ancient Incas of Peru. Tall menhirs on a mountain. But for these what would be left of all that mighty civilization which with its massive stones weighs heavy, like a dark regret, on modern man? Under the mandate of what strange love, what ruthlessness, did that primeval leader of men compel his hordes to drag this temple up the mountainside, bidding them raise up their eternity?... That form

of happiness, those shackles. . . . The leader of those ancient races may have had scant compassion for man's sufferings, but he had a boundless pity for his death. Not for his personal death, but pity for his race, doomed to be blotted out beneath a sea of sand. And so he bade his folk set up these stones at last, something the desert never would engulf" (NF, 262).

35. Nietzsche, *Thus Spoke Zarathustra*, pt. 4, The Song of Melancholy, no. 3, 336: "They pounce on *lambs*, / Headlong down, ravenous, / Lusting for lambs, / Angry at all lamb-souls, / Fiercely angry at all that look / Sheepish, lamb-eyed, curly-woolled, / Grey with lamb-sheep kindliness!" This is what the philosophy of the "eagle natures," "the Flyers," sounds like.

36. CIT, no. 108, 748.

37. CIT, no. 81, 699. E. A. Racky rightly argues that: "The God of Saint-Exupéry is . . . not the God of Christian revelation. Since the author is basically not a believing Christian, he sees God merely as the summit of a hierarchy, to which on a lower level humans also belong. Saint-Exupéry resists the idea of revelation, since he considers a descent of God to the human level as a secularization of the Creator. This explains why Jesus Christ has no place in Saint-Exupéry's work" (*Die Auffassung vom Menschen bei Antoine de Saint-Exupéry*, 86).

Léon Werth declares in his commentary on *Citadelle:* "God cannot be grasped. He answers prayers with silence. . . . He's not an easy-going God, who authorizes our settling down comfortably in faith. . . . A deeply rooted Christian feeling (he often said that his civilization was based on Christian values) is combined with the notion of a harsh kingdom in which sentries who fall asleep are shot" ("Tel que je l'ai connu," in René Delange and Léon Werth, *La vie d'Antoine de Saint-Exupéry*, 159–60).

P. Chevrier, *Saint-Exupéry*, 119, compares his subject's notion of God with the viewpoint of J.-P. Sartre in *The Devil and the Good Lord*, trans. Kitty Black (New York: Knopf, 1960), 141: "You see this emptiness over our heads. This emptiness is God. You see this gap in the door? It is God. Do you see that hole in the ground? That is God again. Silence is God. Absence is God. God is the loneliness of men." In fact Saint-Exupéry's standpoint resembles Sartre's existentialism more closely than it does Christianity (see chap. 6 n. 9 above), but Saint-Exupéry, when he called loneliness "God," felt religious in a certain way, while Sartre ruled out any religious attitudes for himself.

38. See CIT, no. 63, 683: "I stubbornly climbed toward God, to ask him about the meaning of things, and to get him to explain to me where

the exchange that they had tried to impose on me was headed. But on the summit of the mountain I discovered only a heavy block of black granite – and that was God." Luc Estang correctly observes about this "God": "Is he even the God of the philosophers? Not even that, because his transcendence is illusory. He floats in immanence. He does not pre-exist human beings: He is their projection. He is a deistic longing that creates its own object of adoration. . . . For Saint-Exupéry's humanism too, 'God is dead,' but instead of proclaiming this and suggesting a possible replacement, he gives the name of God to the very signs of death: silence and absence. This means acting while 'waiting for Godot' " (*Saint-Exupéry*, 164–65).

Jean-Claude Ibert is right, but only up to a point, when he argues: "As the heir of Pascal and Nietzsche, Saint-Exupéry succeeded in going beyond the Christianity of the one and the atheism of the other. To Nietzsche's (more properly Hegel's) formula, 'God is dead,' he opposes another formula, 'God is silence' " (*Antoine de Saint-Exupéry*, 108; see above chap. 6 n. 24). Saint-Exupéry's clearest statement about his idea of God can be found in his *Notebooks*. There, after a long totting up of the contradictions of Christianity (its intellectual dishonesty, its apodictic dogmatism, etc.) he tersely notes: "What do I care that God doesn't exist? God gives divinity to man" (*Carnets* [Paris: Gallimard, 1953], 40). In other words one has to speak of "God," because "God is the perfect symbolic underpinning of what is at once inaccessible and absolute" (ibid.). "I understand the origin of brotherhood among men. Men were brothers in God. . . . As the inheritor of God, my civilization made men to be brothers in Man" (FTA, 424). What's left is the meaningless husk of the legacy of the Catholic Church: authority, ritual, and sacrifice. "Saint-Exupéry was a God-seeker," writes M. Wicki-Vogt, the German translator of Maria de Crisenoy's *Antoine de Saint-Exupéry*. "He hungered for the bread of the angels" (5). This is true, but Saint-Exupéry was a seeker who was afraid to let himself be found, and a hungry man fearful of being overfed.

39. CIT, no. 213, 978.

40. CIT, no. 2, 517.

41. See Nietzsche: "Even if God no longer exists, the world *shall* be capable of divine creative power, of infinite power to transform" (*Der Wille zur Macht: Versuch einer Umwertung aller Werte*, chosen and arranged by P. Gast and E. Förster-Nietzsche [Stuttgart: Kröner, 1964], no. 1062, 692). "The two most extreme modes of thought – the mechanistic and the Platonic – agree on the eternal return: for both it is an ideal" (ibid., no. 1061, 691).